A Toast – To Whisky

Cheers! – here's the book you've been waiting for. Within, you will find all you wanted to know about Scotch whisky, including how it is made, the colourful history, many redoubtable characters and wild incidents associated with the drink and how to invest in this modern success story, plus a comprehensive guide, details and background to the major malt distilleries.

Exports are currently generating more than £4.5 billion annually for the UK balance of trade, a record high, and 40 bottles a second are shipped abroad, while Scotch now accounts for a quarter of UK food and drinks exports.

There are 108 distilleries in operation in Scotland with 10,000 people directly employed, plus a further 35,000 jobs supported throughout Britain.

Markets are expanding everywhere worldwide, especially in the Far East as the merits of discerning whisky appreciation spreads to different cultures. Vintage and quality are coming once more into their own with the retreat of recession.

So sit down with a neat dram – or indeed any other refreshing libation – and relax, turn the pages at leisure and enjoy... George Forbes

Publisher **Ken Laird**
Lang Syne Publishers Ltd.
79 Main Street, Newtongrange, Midlothian EH22 4NA
Tel: **0131 344 0414**
E Fax: **0845 075 6085**
E-mail: **info@lang-syne.co.uk**
www.langsyneshop.co.uk
Editor **George Forbes**
Writers **George Forbes**
Colin Grant
Design **Dorothy Meikle**
Photography
Alistair Devine
Konrad Borkowski
Dennis Hardley
Print **Warners Midlands plc**

First edition: October, 2013.
Second edition: March 2014.

Secrets of Scotch

The distant, mystical roots of Scotland's (indeed the world's) favourite alcoholic beverage – whisky – have a holy air about them because one pious legend relates how Saint Patrick brought the knack of distilling what the Irish call 'whiskey' (with an 'e') over with him by rowing boat from the Emerald Isle in the sixth century when he visited fellow Christian missionaries in barbaric Caledonia and felt they needed spiritual aid in more ways than one via some ancient and intrinsic Celtic inventiveness.

However, biologists more recently discovered, by examining very old stratified spores and pollen under the microscope, that 'some kind of alcoholic drink' just like whisky had been conjured up by the natives on (suitably enough) the Hebridean island of Rum more than 6,000 years ago which outstrips any Irish saint more than somewhat.

The shivering islanders probably badly needed some kind of strong liquor as a bracing counteragent to the driving rain and bitter winter cold: but whether it was actually real whisky as gratefully imbibed today remains questionable.

Saint Paul in one of his Biblical epistles had made booze respectable by opining that one should 'take wine for thy stomach's sake' but said nothing about fiery spirits, probably because he had never partaken of them under the hot Middle Eastern sun.

However, half a green light to forge ahead regardless of any potential sin was better than none and it was certainly enough laxity to allow monks to enjoy making and tasting their own concoctions, even down to the present day as the Scottish appreciators of Buckfast Tonic Wine, from the Devon abbey of the same name, can gratefully testify.

Whatever the origins and whenever proper whisky making began, the word Scotch has enshrined a particular taste and effect and, thankfully for the Scottish economy, no dogged efforts on the part of American, German or Japanese scientists have ever uncovered that secret element which is more esoteric than that surrounding any other drink.

Scotch is not Rye. It is not Bourbon. It is not all that much like Irish whiskey, though that is the closest apropos ingredients, taste and manufacturing geography.

Why Scotch whisky is so unique will probably and thankfully always remain one of Nature's great unsolved mysteries but it has no doubt something to do with the intermingling of crisp northern air, pure and sometimes daily rainfall engendering bounteous burns and rivers winding down peaty, rocky mountains through the tang of heather, not to mention clammy mists and the copious crops of the Highlands. All of that is fact and nothing to do with advertising copy.

Distilled spirits were given the name aquavitae meaning 'water of life' because they were supposed to have medicinal qualities, probably simply because the liquid tasted like a strong, fiery tonic and certainly acted like a pick-me-up.

The Latin then became 'usqueba' in the Gaelic-speaking wildernesses where it was produced and this in turn was anglified into the more colloquial 'whisky', a description with

Sample testing the malt.

accurate connotations of friskiness, gaiety and warmth as befitting such a restorative beverage with apparently burning, passionate and healing powers.

In fact the healthy effects of whisky may be medically dubious but it certainly made the drinker feel good which was enough for early imbibers to label it a bracing tonic.

The first known reference to Scotch is suitably enough in a receipt for a sale to a jolly monk, one Friar John who bought a quantity of the refreshment for his monastery in 1494, no doubt for the holy mens' stomaches' sakes and to pass many a weary hour.

Farmers with an excess of barley from their crops added to the drink's burgeoning popularity and, the myth of its restorative powers remaining healthy, the Guild of Surgeon Barbers in Edinburgh were allowed to manufacture the drink under licence in 1505 as part of their duties to cater for the well-being of the capital's ever thirsty population.

During the 16th century, distilling became more sophisticated and industrialised and the technique of passing the outlet pipe through cold, running water was introduced via the copper worm, the latter, as its name suggests, being a large, spiral, elongated funnel through which evaporated alcohol was condensed into liquid form.

The pear-shaped still was also introduced which strained off obnoxious substances and, by the mid-16th century, efficient whisky making was firmly established.

There was even concern around this time that the production of basic food was being adversely affected by the whisky making process which diverted increasing amounts of the autumn harvest from more normal products. This testifies to the growing popularity of whisky.

Needless to say, all this prosperity allied to jollity could not

Global fight on fakes

Scotch Whisky is a 'geographical indication', meaning it can only be produced in Scotland. It has been defined in UK legislation since 1933.

It is obviously in the interests of Scotch Whisky producers to stop companies overseas taking unfair advantage of the reputation of Scotch Whisky. A consequence of the success of Scotch Whisky - £4.3 billion in exports in 2012 – is that there are many who will try to sell fake 'Scotch Whiskies'.

The Scotch Whisky Association (SWA) has been litigating since the early 1950s to protect Scotch Whisky. Usually it takes civil legal action in the courts, but its lawyers also work with the administrative and criminal authorities in overseas markets. For example, the Chinese Administration of Industry and Commerce have been very co-operative in taking action to stop the sale of fake 'Scotch Whisky' in China.

Not only does the sale of each fake deprive a Scotch Whisky producer of a sale, but, as fakes are usually of poor quality, it will damage the reputation of Scotch Whisky with consumers.

The SWA relies on reports from members and their distributors, embassies, investigators, local lawyers and members of the public alerting it to fakes.

The aim of the SWA legal department is to ensure that, when consumers buy Scotch Whisky all over the world, they receive the genuine product. We have a lot of success in tracking down fakes and work well with authorities in markets around the world to ensure the issue is kept under control.

If a consumer buys Scotch Whisky in a reputable store they should not be overly concerned about the possibility of it being a fake. However, if a consumer has a concern they can raise it directly with the SWA or the relevant authorities.

The SWA over the years has authorised legal action against over 1,000 brands and nearly 3,000 trademarks worldwide have been opposed. Today, at any one time, up to 70 different legal actions around the world are being pursued.

Rosemary Gallagher,
SWA communications manager

go unpunished and the first excise duty (2/8d per pint) was imposed in 1544 by the Scottish Parliament of the time, ostensibly to help finance the nation's army: but one can also picture those dour, puritan administrators deciding with shaking heads that there was just too much enjoyment and laxity going on.

By the 18th century there were large, legitimate and efficient distilleries dotted throughout Scotland, as well as countless illicit private stills up in the hills or hidden on the moors, the uncovering of which kept the dreaded, uniformed and armed excisemen busy.

The problem with the supposedly civilised central belt of Scotland was that for many Highlanders there was nothing wrong about making their own spirits which were a gift of Nature after all and a blessing from God on what could often be a bleak landscape.

It was in their blood and in a roundabout way even had Biblical sanction via Saint Paul.

This heritage of making their own moonshine was taken by Highland emigrants to the United States and was most graphically enacted amid the backwoods of Kentucky and Tennessee where hillbillies of Celtic descent defied federal agents well into the middle of last century, displays of nonconformity which often involved hair raising car chases along winding country roads.

The royal seal of approval was bestowed on the national beverage of Scotland by King George IV in 1822 when he made the first regal visit by a reigning British monarch north of the border in more than a century.

This grand occasion was meticulously masterminded by Sir Walter Scott who made sure that all the official ceremonies were suitably bedecked in tartanalia. ▶

The Scotch Whisky industry is involved in a range of initiatives to promote responsible attitudes to alcohol and tackle alcohol related harm.

As a drink created only after years of quiet maturation, Scotch Whisky is a drink to be sipped and savoured. The industry wishes its consumers to enjoy its products responsibly.

When the royal yacht docked at Leith (near the present site of the permanently berthed royal yacht 'Britannia'), the King suitably and diplomatically toasted Scott in a glass of the best Highland malt.

The renowned novelist then asked to keep the glass as a memento, placing it delicately in his hip pocket but later forgetting about it and sitting down with a startled yell, alarming the regal bodyguard as the broken glass cut into his ample behind.

The delicate art of blending (combining grain and malt strains into a golden, glowing liquid) was first introduced by Andrew Usher in Edinburgh in 1860 and proved so popular that sales at home and abroad soared: but by then whisky had become a way of life and part of national culture as Highlanders and Islanders flocked down to the Lowlands for more lucrative employment during the Industrial Revolution, bringing their traditions and drinking habits from remote bothies to busy city hostelries where such merrymaking has remained entrenched down to the present day.

Whisky, with its raucous reputation for making social gatherings go with an uninhibited swing, became a staple of jaunty public occasions whether the event was a wedding, a christening, a birthday, a stag or hen night, a banquet, a reunion or just an average party. It even became an emotional bulwark at funerals.

During Prohibition in America, smuggled whisky more than doubled in value and many a lucrative boatload was shipped over and landed on the East Coast on moonless nights. The expression 'the real McCoy', to denote the genuine article, originated at this time and was taken from a captain of the same name who made a good living in this illicit trade because he supplied speakeasies with authentic whisky instead of bootleg slop.

In some remote Scottish crofts in the far north well into last century whisky was still consumed as a bracer for the day ahead as it had been from time immemorial. Regardless of its supposed healthy propensities, a quaff of it certainly felt good, especially on cold winter mornings.

Perhaps some solemn stone monument should be erected one day on top of Ben Nevis dedicated to 'the Unknown Distiller known only to God' whoever he was, whether saint or monk, farmer or landowner, the first pioneer who concocted the original dram who is well worth commemorating if anyone is.

For as the poet Robert Burns, himself an enthusiastic imbiber of 'the cratur', once wrote of Scotland's favourite tipple -
Inspiring bold John Barleycorn,
What dangers thou canst make us scorn!
Wi' tippenny we fear nae evil;
W' usquabae we'll face the Devil!

George Forbes

The spirit safe allows the distiller to analyse and manage the product of the spirit still without ever coming into contact with the spirit itself. It dates back to 1823 when the duty laws were changed to allow small Highland distilleries to compete on equal terms with the large Lowland distilleries.

The last time I turned down a whisky,
I didn't understand the question. – *anon*

Whisky is the cure
for which there is
no disease.
– *anon*

Whisky is liquid
sunshine. – *George
Bernard Shaw,
playwright*

I should never have switched from
Scotch to Martinis. – *Hollywood legend
Humphrey Bogart's last words...*

A good gulp of whisky at bedtime –
its not very scientific, but it helps.
*– Sir Alexander Fleming
(discoverer of penicillin, 1881-1955)*

I always take Scotch whisky at night
as a preventative of toothache.
I have never had the toothache;
and what is more I never intend to have it.
– Mark Twain, American writer

Whisky 12 Key Facts

What is Scotch whisky?

It is a distillate exclusively made in Scotland from the elements of native cereals, water and yeast. A distillate is the end result when a process takes place which through boiling methods evaporates a liquid and then condenses its vapour, purifying it and separating key elements by using various heating methods, thus ending up with an extracted essence, in this case malt whisky.

What is a single whisky?

The product of a single distillery. Some distilleries produce their output primarily for the purpose of blending with others while many retain their production for sale as single whiskies. A single malt is the product of one malt whisky distillery and a single grain is the product of one grain whisky distillery.

Why is Irish whiskey spelt differently?

This is simply a convention of language that grew commonplace over the centuries which was used to differentiate Irish whiskey from Scotch whisky.

What is the difference between Scotch, Irish and American or Canadian whiskies?

The differences are obviously geographical but also in the method of production. Scotch for instance is made and matured in Scotland using malted barley in pot stills, whereas American Bourbon whiskey is made and matured in the United States from a mash of corn grain.

What are spirits?

This describes the product of distillation.

How many distilleries in Scotland are there?

This has varied over the centuries depending on the country's economic situation and agricultural factors but on average there have been around a hundred operating annually. Some of these have been mothballed for years, going in and out of production.

Ballantine's – a fine example of a blend.

Can Scotch whisky only be made in Scotland?

Yes and this is legally enforceable. Other products have been copied abroad but not Scotch which is unique to the land where it is made.

What is blending?

Many distilleries sell part of their product as single or unblended whiskies: but their whiskies are also used to make up well-known brands of blended whiskies. Blending is the art, acquired after years of experience, of combining whiskies from several different distilleries, malt as well as grain. A blend consists of from 15 to 50 single whiskies combined in the recipe proportions of a formula that is the secret of the blending company concerned and the end product is then sold under a world famous brand name. Just as in other walks of life, the various flavours have to be chosen carefully to make sure they are compatible.

Is it legal to sell whisky which is less than three years old in Britain?

No. The product does not qualify as Scotch whisky unless it has matured for a minimum of three years.

How many brands of Scotch whisky are there?

Similar to the number of distilleries, there are around a hundred well known brands on the home market but many more are sold under different names abroad or sold to individuals or private organisations.

At what temperature is whisky best served?

There are no rules about this. Room temperature is normal.

At what strength is whisky sold at home and for export?

Most whiskies retail at 40% volume of alcohol for the home market. A strength of 43% volume is normally preferred for export markets. This is roughly the same as brandy, gin and rum but higher than vodka.

Aberfeldy

Aberfeldy, Perthshire PH15 2EB.

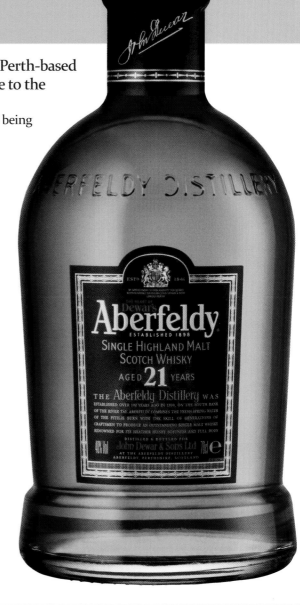

Built over a two-year period and opened in 1898 by the Perth-based blenders John Dewar and Sons, this distillery lies close to the River Tay.

One of the founders, Tommy Dewar, a sporty type, achieved fame as being just the third person in Britain to buy a motor car, then the latest in fashionable accoutrements for aristocrats (even though he was more nouveau riche in trade than blue blooded). However, the image always helped the brand.

Major rebuilding took place at the distillery in 1972 with four stills being constructed.

The water source is the local Pitillie Burn and more than 2,100,000 litres of whisky are produced here annually. This malt is a major contributor to the popular Dewar blends.

The site of the distillery was once close to a colony of rare red squirrels and the area generally is renowned for its wildlife.

In 2000 the Dewars World of Whisky Visitors' Centre was opened at the distillery which will tell you all you want to know about the product.

The months of October and November are known as 'the silent season' because the distillery is closed to visitors while maintenance work goes on but the brand centre, store and coffee shop remain open.

The nearby town of Aberfeldy, which gives the whisky its name, lies on one of General Wade's roads used by the redcoats to subjugate the rebellious Highlanders.

Another military connection is the statue of kilted soldiers in the town which commemorates the first gathering of the famous Black Watch regiment in 1839. No doubt they toasted future victories with the best local malts.

Another spot was made famous by Robert Burns in his celebrated poem 'The Birks of Aberfeldy' and he, an appreciator of whisky, also probably sampled the local spirit before becoming inspired.

Visiting: +44 (0) 1887 822010.

Tasting Notes

This dram stimulates a veritable cornucopia of fruity tastes on the pallet. There are traces and hints of all kinds of flavours here, including oranges, spices and pineapples: but the final result is pleasingly dry to the discerning taste.

Aberfeldy Distillery.

The still room.

Aberlour

Aberlour-on-Spey, Banffshire AB38 9PJ.

This is most renowned as a 12 year-old single malt. The distillery, which produces more than two million litres of spirits annually, is built in a romantic setting at the foot of Ben Rinnes, five miles south west of Dufftown in west Banffshire, where the Lour Burn joins the River Spey.

It is in the middle of Scotland's whisky making country and is one of the more famous sites in an area celebrated by lovers of spirits worldwide. The crystal clear water from local burns that gurgle happily down the mountain are used in the distilling process to give that extra tang to the product.

The building was founded in 1879 on the site of an ancient distillery which in the distant past produced illicit spirits. It has been considerably modernized over the years, especially after two bad fires.

The name Aberlour is descriptive of the site, meaning 'mouth of the chattering burn' and the whisky is currently owned by Pernod Ricard.

The product's suitable slogan is 'where the past lingers in the present' thus conveying the message that ancient secrets and recipes are passed down through the generations.

This whisky is smooth and aromatic and is best drunk after a good dinner. The best vintages are 10, 12, 15, 18, 21 and 22 years old.

In 1973 two more stills were added to make four in total at a time when whisky was becoming more popular worldwide, thanks to the opening up of new markets, most notably in the Far East.

At the distillery there is a celebrated connoisseurs tour which finishes with a nosing and tasting of five spirits and a chance to fill your own bottle, complete with a personalised label.

Aberlour has won five gold medals at international wine and spirit competitions over the past few years putting it well into the forefront of the best malts.

Visiting: +44 (0) 1340 881249.

The Aberlour Distillery.

Labelling the Aberlour by hand.

Tasting Notes

Autumn is the season that holds sway over this dram which is velvety sweet with traces of honey and nutmeg. It is warming and soft and full of mellow fruitfulness, just as Keats once described autumn.

Abhainn Dearg

Carnish, Isle of Lewis, Outer Hebrides HS2 9EX.

The current owner is Mark Tayburn and the licence for this distillery was granted by HM Revenue and Customs as late as November, 2008, which makes it one of the newest distilleries in the land. The water sources are local springs but the official annual capacity of this distillery has not been released as yet.

The name Abhainn Dearg means Red River in Gaelic.

In 2011 the first single malt was released: but there are no bottlings on an industrial scale as yet.

This is the first malt to be manufactured on Lewis since 1840, though the area used to be rich in small, unauthorized stills, as were all the Western Isles.

It was easy at first for the old islanders to manufacture their own whisky for home use well away from the clutches of law enforcers stationed on the mainland and later to transport such illicit goods wherever smugglers wanted.

However, the clampdown on Lewis by the customs and excise authorities was so thorough and drastic that it really curtailed any whisky making at all, unlike Islay where official distilleries soon flourished and took the place of illegal stills.

Carnish, where Abhainn Dearg is based, should not be confused with Callanish, also on the island, which is famed for its Bronze Age standing stones, a Hebridean version of Stonehenge.

Visiting: +44 (0) 1851 672429.

Abhainn Dearg Distillery.

Tasting Notes

A typical Hebridean dram with a refreshing feel of the great outdoors about it, not to mention the energetic drive of tidal waves coming off the North Atlantic. A mildly herbal flavour with just a hint of pears rounds off the experience.

Abhainn Dearg stills.

Ailsa Bay

Girvan, Ayrshire KA26 9PT.

The current owners of this distillery are William Grant and Sons Ltd. The source of water is the nearby quaintly-named Penwapple reservoir and this distillery produces five million litres of malt whisky annually.

Building began in 2007 and two years later it was officially opened by Prince Charles.

Situated next door to the Girvan grain distillery, this malt distillery is also close to the site of the old and now defunct Ladyburn Distillery which pioneered whisky making in this area.

There are no bottlings as yet but be patient, they will come.

This part of the Clyde coast may not usually be associated with distilling in the public mind but at Campbeltown on the Mull of Kintyre opposite across the Firth there were at one time 14 distilleries in operation.

Ailsa Craig, which gives Ailsa Bay whisky its name, is a craggy rock rising to 1,114 feet a dozen miles south of Arran, where granite used to be quarried to make curling stones. There is no Ailsa Bay listed on any directory but it sounds nice and atmospheric.

Ailsa Bay Distillery is named after Ailsa Craig.

Tasting Notes

As smooth as honey, this dram benefits, as so many others do, from the addition of fresh Scottish water which brings out underlying flavours of yeast and oatmeal which in turn give a bittersweet emphasis to the imbibing process.

There are two things a Highlander likes naked and one of them is malt whisky. – *Scottish Proverb*

Ardbeg

Port Ellen, Isle of Islay PA42 7EA.

The current owners of this distillery are Glenmorangie plc. The water sources are two local lochs and the distillery produces a million litres of malt whisky annually.

In the late 18th century, smugglers were distilling illicit whisky on this site and taking it via their small sailing ships by the barrel-load to unload on moonless nights via deserted beaches along the Scottish coastline. The whisky was hidden in caves and distributed inland by way of teams of pack horses and donkeys.

By 1815 the army redcoats plus armed customs and excise officers had taken a firmer grip of the situation, the islands being the last place where lawlessness was stamped out, and officially approved whisky-making introduced.

The local MacDougall family, some of whose extended and extensive members had been involved in smuggling in the past, saw which way the wind was blowing and founded a proper distillery which became fully operational by 1817.

The Ardbeg Distillery Limited was not officially created, however, until 1959. They always took things slowly in the islands, even more slowly than in the Highlands.

In 1977 the distillery was acquired by Hiram Walker who closed it down after only four years of production.

In 1989 it was taken over by Allied Distillers and production recommenced.

In 1997 the distillery was acquired by the present owners and a year later a new visitors centre was opened, a certain signal it was here to stay this time.

Ardbeg no longer malts its own barley but buys in some ingredients for what is considered to be the most heavily-peated malt in Scotland.

Ardbeg's best vintages are ten and seventeen years old.

Visiting: +44 (0) 1496 302244.

Tasting Notes

Reminiscent of freshly dug island peat on a cold winter's morn, this dram packs a punch and is strong and reliable. A typical product of Islay much appreciated by aficionados of this branch of whisky production, the malt is smoky with an underlying memory of dried fruits.

Ardbeg Distillery.

Ardmore

Kennethmont, Huntly, Aberdeenshire AB54 4NH.

This distillery is currently owned by Fortune Brands Inc. The water sources are springs up on nearby Knockandy Hill and the distillery produces 5,100,000 litres of malt whisky annually.

It was built in 1899 by William Teacher and Sons.

In 1958 an extra pair of stills were added and in 1975 a further four. The following year the plant was taken over by Allied Brewers, now Allied Distillers.

In 1999 a 12-year-old malt was released to commemorate the distillery's anniversary and four years later it was taken over by the present owners.

This distillery has its own, now disused, cooperage.

The malt was a major component of Teacher's Highland Cream which was only fitting since they had founded the distillery in the first place.

Kennethmont, where the distillery is based, is a village in north west Aberdeenshire, seven miles south of Huntly.

Aberdeen is now so much associated with

The beautiful copper-domed, cast iron mash tun has long been a fixture of the distillery and is the envy of the industry.

North Sea oil that the public forget the thriving distilling industry which has been a feature of the crop-rich hinterland of Aberdeenshire for centuries.

The county also borders more renowned and celebrated 'whisky counties' and is part of that north east shoulder of Scotland which is made up of farmlands, mountains and streams, all geographic features integral to the folklore, mystique and production of malt whisky.

Visiting: +44 (0) 1464 831213.

Ardmore Distillery.

Tasting Notes

The timeless ghost of the peat fire flame can be detected in this dram made additionally zestful by an input of citrus fruits. It lingers in the senses long after sampling. Very relaxing.

Mashing in: The mash tun holds a fulsome 12.5 tonnes!

Arran

Lochranza, Isle of Arran KA27 8HJ.

The current owners of this distillery are Isle of Arran Distillers Ltd. The water source is Loch na Davie and the output of this distillery is 750,000 litres annually, making it one of the country's smallest with regards to production.

In 1997 a visitors centre opened and two years later the first three-year-old vintage was released.

In 2006 the Arran ten-year-old vintage was also released.

The last legal distillery on the island was closed in 1836.

The picturesque island of Arran's close proximity to the mainland makes it an ideal spot for the production and distribution of whisky since it is part of the western seaboard while also retaining strong links to various distribution points in urban Scotland.

Broddick Castle on the Isle of Arran.

There is no tradition of whisky making on Arran which lies in the Firth of Clyde, 14 miles from the mainland to the east and just four miles from the Kintyre peninsula to the west.

It has sometimes been called the Tahiti of the Western Isles with its mountainous interior, quiet golden beaches and palm trees: but it certainly has all the ingredients for whisky making, including fertile fields and rocky streams.

It has also been labelled Scotland in microcosm, so there is no reason why the national drink should not take a proper foothold as well.

Visiting: +44 (0) 1770 830264.

Maturing nicely.

Tasting Notes

The additional dash of clear, crystal water brings out a taste of apricots and cloves, with further hints of malt, caramel and nuts, all underlined by suggestions of the sherry casks in which the malt was matured.

The Isle of Arran Distillery on Open Day.

Auchentoshan

Dalmuir, Dunbartonshire G81 4SJ.

The current owners of this distillery are Morrison Bowmore, who in turn are owned by Japanese conglomerate Suntory. The water source is Cochna Loch in the Kilpatrick Hills overlooking the Clyde and this distillery produces 1,650,000 litres of malt whisky annually.

It was founded in 1823 and acquired in the 1960s by Glasgow brewers Tennants.

In 1974 Eadie Cairns Ltd. took over the business and re-equipped the premises.

In 1984 it was acquired by the present owners who ten years later were bought over by Suntory acting as the parent company.

In 2004 a new visitors' centre was opened.

Auchentoshan means 'corner of the field' in Gaelic and this plant uses an unusual triple distillation process.

Vintages which are best are 10, 21, 22 and 25 years old.

This distillery is unusual in Scottish whisky making in that it lies close to Glasgow and the industrial lowlands. Its very address – Dalmuir – is of a suburb in the west of the city.

However, as any Glaswegian will tell you, a stroll round the Kilpatrick Hills, where the whisky has its water source, is just like being in the Highlands.

Indeed just a few miles further westwards lies Loch Lomond which is really where the Highlands begin and what was known as the Highland Line, which bisected the mountains from the plains, runs through this area.

So, although not technically in the Highlands, the Auchentoshan distillery is not too far away; and all the ingredients are there for a good malt, including good local farmlands along the banks of the River Clyde plus streams coming down from the high hills and the occasional rockbound loch.

The distillery also proves that such establishments need not be placed in the wilder parts of the country and, rather like oil prospecting, there are possibilities in Scotland's semi-rural landscape, in the lowlands, of developing whisky-making on a larger scale.

Visiting: +44 (0) 1389 878561.

Auchentoshan Distillery.

Auchentoshan warehouse.

Tasting Notes

With a hint of freshly plucked raspberries, this malt can actually taste marshmallowy with a trace of nuts and even liquorice if water is added. Sometimes criticised as tasting medicinal, it can certainly act as a tonic on any dull day.

Auchroisk

Mulben, Banffshire AB55 6XS.

Auchroisk Distillery.

The current owners are Justerini and Brookes Ltd., a subsidiary of UDV. The water source is the nearby Dories Well (which hopefully will never run dry) and the output of this distillery is 3,100,000 litres of malt whisky annually.

This is a modern plant established in 1974 which began production a year later.

In 2001 the name Singleton of Auchroisk was abandoned and the brand Auchroisk 10-year-old was launched.

The distillery is based four miles west of Keith in Banffshire, a county synonymous with whisky making since in the middle of last century, when there was a boom in malt whisky consumption which has continued ever since. At one time there were 25 fully operational distilleries in the area.

Banffshire is a wedge-shaped county which is ten miles wide in the south and broadens to 31 miles of the Moray Firth coastline in the north and has a disproportionate amount of distilleries within its boundaries, relative to its size of just 403,054 acres.

But it had all the geographical assets necessary in the production of whisky, namely a mountainous interior, rich farmlands and many clear streams and fast flowing rivers. Among the latter are the Avon, Deveron, Isla and Spey, all of whose waters are vital ingredients in many whiskies, with Speyside in particular being renowned for the distilleries along its banks.

Visiting: +44 (0) 1542 860333.

Tasting Notes

Peaches and oranges are never too far away from the taste buds in this mellow malt which also has flavours of figs and ginger to add to its bouquet.

Friendship is like whisky, The older the better. – *Anon*

Aultmore

Keith, Banffshire AB55 3QY.

Being on the popular tourist Whisky Trail, Aultmore is owned by John Dewar and Sons. The water source is the Burn of Auchindorran and it produces 2,100,000 litres of malt annually.

Built in 1896 by Alexander Forres, the owner of Benrinnes Distillery, this neighbouring distillery was sold to Dewars in 1923.

At the first go they only held on to it for two years before selling it to the Distillers Company who then passed it on to Scottish Malt Distillers five years later.

In 1970 the entire distillery was renovated and extended from two to four stills then sold to the Bacardi company in 1998 who by that time had become the parent company of Dewars, such being the changing cosmopolitan tastes of the drinking public.

Aultmore in Gaelic means 'Big Burn' and the malt has been a long time contributor to Dewars' blends.

It is best known for its 12-year-old malt which has become increasingly popular.

In common with many other malts, this brand only came before the Scottish drinking public's gaze in recent decades.

Not that long ago – at least up to the 1960s – an older generation in the big cities would only have thought of whisky in terms of blends, so that malts, if thought about at all, would be dismissed as mere contributors to these common, yellowish spirits.

Whisky was never pale or clear for a long time in urban areas and it was only with more discerning, sophisticated tastes in the 1960s that malts came into their own as palates became more refined. **Visiting: +44 (0) 1542 882762.**

Circa 1890s.

THE AULTMORE-GLENLIVET DISTILLERY.

Aultmore Distillery today.

The still house.

Aultmore Distillery circa 1950s.

Tasting Notes

Crisp and delicate, shot through with fresh fruits, this malt after a hearty quaff ends up dry but fresh in the mouth. Clean, crisp and delicate are the suitable adjectives to describe rounding off the sampling experience.

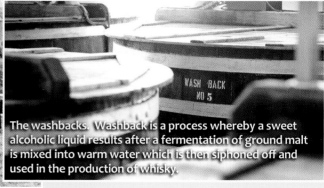

The washbacks. Washback is a process whereby a sweet alcoholic liquid results after a fermentation of ground malt is mixed into warm water which is then siphoned off and used in the production of whisky.

Balblair

Edderton, Tain, Ross-shire IV19 1LB.

This is most renowned as a five-year-old Highland malt. Built in 1790 on the site of a distillery founded 40 years previously, this building lies within a quarter of a mile of the Dornoch Firth and near ancient Pictish standing stones, the area being renowned for its ancient archaeology.

All the local streams provide excellent water running through peat which may explain why this whisky can be drunk unusually young for a malt.

The main source for water is a burn called the Allt Dearg and the distillery produces 1,330,000 litres of whisky annually.

Currently owned by Inver House Distillers, this building was closed from 1911 to 1949 and during the Second World War it was commandeered by the army with no doubt the squaddies wishing it was still in working order.

With the upturn in the spirits market generally, upgrading took place in 1964 and a steam boiler was installed.

The Balblair 33-year-old product was first bottled in 2000 and three years later it won a gold medal in the International Wine and Spirit competition.

The Balblair 38-year-old malt was first 'released' in 2004 and the brand name has increased sales by 25% this century, being a bit of a late starter because of the closure earlier in the 20th century, a delay which production has more than made up for.

It is one of Scotland's oldest distilleries and is situated in a scenic part of the country where the Ross-shire streams flow down the Struie Hill to the farmlands of Edderton, known colloquially as 'the parish of the peats', and then burble onwards down to the rolling, welcoming waves of the Dornoch Firth.

Visiting: contact www.balblair.com

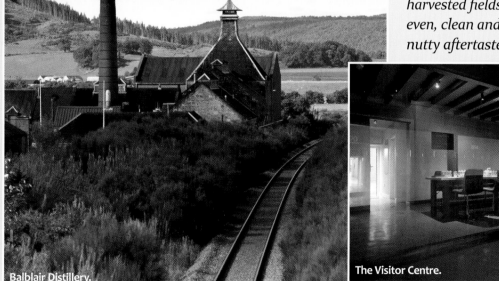

Balblair Distillery.

Tasting Notes

Light and fresh with a suggestion of harvested fields, this dram is normally even, clean and delicate with a slightly nutty aftertaste.

The Visitor Centre.

17

Balmenach

Cromdale, Moray PH26 3PF.

The distillery was first established by local entrepreneur James McGregor in 1824. It was purchased by the Balmenach-Glenlivet Distillery Company in 1897. In 1930 the Scottish Malt Distillers company took over and the premises were closed in 1941 to be reopened six years later after the war had ended and rationing was eased.

In 1962 another pair of stills were added to the existing four.

In 1968 the mash house was entirely renovated.

In 1993 it was mothballed by United Distillers then four years later acquired and reopened by the present owners, Inver House Distillers.

The source of water is springs running down the nearby Cromdale Hills and 1,800,000 litres of malt whisky are produced here annually.

Grantown on Spey. The Balmenach Distillery in Cromdale lies between Grantown-on-Spey and Aberlour.

This distillery was a major contributor to Johnnie Walker blends.

It was also one of the first legal distilleries sanctioned by government legislation which was passed a year before it was built in the village of Cromdale, one of the traditional crossing points on the River Spey.

Atop a hill nearby stand the ruins of an old castle where in 1690 fleeing Jacobites took refuge after their defeat at the battle on the Haughs of Cromdale. They probably longed for a soothing dram at the time.

Inver House Distillers have not yet mass produced a single malt bottling from this distillery but a limited number of bottles of Balmenach 27 and 28-year-old malts have been produced for their Highland Selection, a range of limited edition single malts which have been individually selected by managers from five distilleries.

Visiting: +44 (0) 1479 872569.

Tasting Notes

A dash of water is recommended to take away the sharpness of the taste. Comparatively rare, this malt is still worth seeking out with its distinctively pungent flavour of peat smoke.

A 'whisky train' on Speyside in 1951. The wagons contained thousands of bottles from local distilleries for export worldwide.

Balvenie

Dufftown, Banffshire AB55 4BB.

The owners of this distillery are William Grant and Sons Ltd, the water source is the nearby Robbie Dubh burn and 5,600,000 litres of malt are produced annually, making it one of the most productive outlets in Scotland.

It was built in 1892 alongside its sister distillery, Glenfiddich, by Grant and Sons, making it one of the few remaining distilleries which have stayed under the same independent ownership since its inception.

In 1957 the stills were doubled from two to four in anticipation of an upturn in trade; and, with the success of this innovation, two more stills were added eight years later.

In 1971 another still was added.

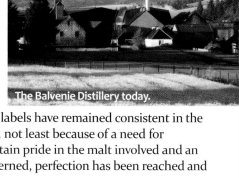
The Balvenie Distillery today.

In 1993 there was a change of bottle design from an unusual brandy carafe style to a more traditional whisky style.

In general the shapes of bottles and their labels have remained consistent in the whisky marketing business over the decades, not least because of a need for recognition. The other aim was to show a certain pride in the malt involved and an indication that, as far as the makers are concerned, perfection has been reached and nothing more need be done.

It is the opposite of the modern trend for ever changing fads and fashions and is none the worse for that.

Balvenie is also one of only a few distilleries to have its own working floor maltings.

Much of the barley used comes from the Grant family farm nearby, the Mains of Balvenie.

This malt is renowned for its 10, 12, 15, 21 and 30-year-old vintages.

Balvenie has been the winner of several gold and silver medals at international competitions from the 1990s onwards and this brand remains traditional – with local produce and long-term ownership.

This goes for much of the whisky making industry where the time honoured advice – if it ain't broke, don't mend it – was never more true.

Visiting: +44 (0) 1340 822210.

Tasting Notes

Sweet sherry, spices, cinnamon and even a hint of a banana flavour lurk in the background of this malt's taste. Full bodied and rich, there is also a flavour of peat and the general effect it produces has been compared to being warm and relaxed by a blazing Highland fireplace on a wintry night.

The Balvenie is the only distillery to maintain and operate a working floor maltings in the Scottish Highlands. After steeping the grain in spring water sourced from the hills above the distillery, the grains are spread across the malting floor. The barley warms up as it starts to germinate and needs to do so evenly. Four malt men turn it up to four times a day until it's ready for the kiln. Here it is dried using anthracite and a carefully judged amount of peat, which adds further complexity to the whisky.

The Distillery in the 1920s.

19

Ben Nevis

Lochy Bridge, Fort William PH33 6TJ.

This distillery was founded by 'Long John' Macdonald in 1825 and, in an early example of shrewd promotion, a cask was presented to Queen Victoria when she visited Fort William in 1848.

The water for this whisky comes from a stream known as the Mill Burn and it produces two million litres annually.

The malt is also renowned as 'the dew of Ben Nevis', Britain's highest mountain at 4,406 ft. above sea level.

A special still was installed in 1955 which allowed for the production of both malt and grain whiskies simultaneously.

In 1990 the process reverted solely to the production of malt whiskies.

The best vintages are 10, 15, 25 and 26 years old.

As its name suggests nearby Fort William, dominating the entrance to the Great Glen, was of strategic importance for controlling the Highlands and the first fort was built there by General Monk in 1654, being expanded after the 1745 Jacobite Rebellion by General Wade.

The fort was eventually demolished to make way for a railway station which in turn has been, in typical modernist fashion, replaced by a lochside bypass and a supermarket.

Fort William is now a tourist hub for those wishing to explore the Highlands. Ben Nevis malt is fondly imbibed at the many hotels and taverns that make up this wee toon. The liquid plays a traditional part in supplying good, warming Scottish hospitality to the wayfarer just as it has for centuries supplied rejuvenation for all those on the road in this wild stretch of the country.

Visiting: +44 (0) 1397 702476.

Tasting Notes

A springy freshness allied to a medium-sweet, soft smokiness with a suggestion of tannin combine to make up the tasting experience.

Ben Nevis Distillery.

The mountain dominates the area.

BenRiach

Longmorn, Near Elgin, Morayshire IV30 8SJ.

The current owners are the BenRiach Distillery Company Ltd. The water source is the nearby Burnside Springs and 2,800,000 litres of malt are produced annually.

The plant was established in 1898 by the Grant family on the same site as their Longmorn Distillery.

However, after just two years of production the BenRiach premises was partly mothballed due to the whisky industry in general moving into one of its periodic times of recession.

Though parts of the distillery remained closed for the next 65 years (a record for a now flourishing business), its floor maltings remained in constant production, providing malted barley for the fully operational adjacent Longmorn Distillery.

In 1965 the BenRiach plant was fully reopened by Glenlivet Distilleries Ltd., having been almost completely rebuilt and refurbished.

By contrast, many of the distilleries closed in 1900, a bad year for the industry, have never been reopened and in some cases have been demolished.

In 1972 the production of peated malt whisky began, using the distillery's own peated Speyside malt on site.

In 1978 Seagrams bought the business.

In 1985 two stills were added to make a total of four.

BenRiach was then released for the first time as a single malt brand in its own right, being bottled as ten years old.

Seagrams was acquired in 2001 by the French firm Pernod Ricard.

The distillery was mothballed for a couple of years before being acquired and reopened by an independent consortium in 2004.

Vintage brands which had been maturing for 21, 25 and 30 years were then launched over the next few years and the whisky has gone from strength to strength ever since.

Visiting: +44 (0) 1343 862888.

BenRiach Distillery.

Tasting Notes

Summer berries and spices stimulate the taste buds when it comes to sampling this malt which also divulges in its tender mixture hints of cinnamon and sweet sherry.

The still house.

21

Benromach

Invererne Road, Forres, Morayshire IV36 3EB.

The current owners are Gordon and MacPhail. The water source is the Chapeltown Springs near Forres and 500,000 litres of whisky are produced annually from the Benromach Distillery.

Whisky was first made here in the final year of the 19th century but this imposing building, lying on the outskirts of the Royal Burgh and ancient

Inspecting the the washback.

market town of Forres, lay silent and empty for years. It has now has been transformed and revived by its present owners.

It was established by a spirit broker from Leith and a distiller from the Glen Nevis plant and passed through various hands until being largely rebuilt in 1966 by Scottish Malt Distillers with two new stills being added a dozen years later.

It was purchased by the present owners in the 1990s and more renovation work involved the installation of two more stills.

The Benromach Distillery was officially opened by the Prince of Wales in 1998 and the new Malt Whisky Centre opened a year later, a suitable location for such an attraction, being in the centre of Speyside, traditional malt making country.

Visiting: +44 (0) 1309 675968.

Benromach Distillery.

Tasting Notes

This can prove a complex tasting experience with wood smoke competing against citrus fruits on the palate. It is a heartening dram with a spicy tang in an aftertaste which lasts a long, reassuring time.

Distillery Manager, Keith Cruickshank checking the spirit safe.

Bladnoch

Wigtown, Galloway, DG8 9AB.

With its position as the most southerly distillery in Scotland, this venture lies in an area steeped in tales of smugglers and poets. Established in 1817 by Thomas McClelland and nestling a mile south east of Wigtown, the county capital, its fortunes have been as choppy as the nearby coast.

Wigtown is built on a hill overlooking a bay where smugglers' boats used to ferry illicit Scotch liquor across the treacherous Solway Firth, with its deceptive quicksands, to England where such cargoes were always warmly welcomed.

The poet Robert Burns, a great celebrator and imbiber of whisky of whom modern public relations experts would have been proud, was very familiar with this area and a frequent patron of its many convivial taverns.

Plentiful streams help with the distilling process, with the key water source being the crisp and clear River Bladnoch, which allows the distillery to produce 250,000 litres of malt whisky annually.

In 1929 the operation succumbed to the worldwide trade depression which lasted throughout what became known as the Hungry Thirties.

It was resurrected in 1956 when the Bladnoch Distillery Co. Ltd. was formed. It proved so successful that ten years later another pair of stills were added to the original two.

In 1973 it was sold to Inverhouse Distillers and in 1993 it was mothballed. Two years later it was sold to the current owners, Raymond Armstrong of Northern Ireland, whose own distillery lies just a few miles across the Irish Channel from Galloway. Limited production began from 2000.

Visiting: +44 (0) 1988 402605.

Barrels stored at the distillery.

Tasting Notes

Retaining a sweet aftertaste from the Bourbon casks in which it is matured, this dram is suitably golden, given a boost by scents of almonds and even damp grass, a commodity in which Scotland abounds. An addition of water brings out the underlying scent of wildflowers.

Bladnoch Distillery with its distinctive pagoda, the latter resembling, as its nickname suggests, a Far Eastern, towered temple.

Bladnoch Bridge.

Blair Athol

Perth Road, Pitlochry, Perthshire PH16 5LY.

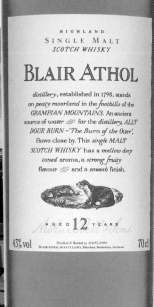

This is most celebrated as an eight-year-old Highland single malt. The distillery was licensed in 1825 on the site of an older one. Arthur Bell and Sons bought it in 1933 and the building is set in picturesque surroundings with colourful gardens full of rhododendrons and roses in summer.

The distillery is kept busy producing 2,300,000 litres annually.

The first references to a distillery here are in records dating back to 1798.

Following a downturn in business generally, the distillery was closed between 1932 and 1949. It was not reopened until major renovation had taken place after which the malt became a contributing ingredient to Bell's blends, the latter made famous by its advertising slogan 'afore ye go!'

In 1973 the number of stills was increased from two to four.

In 1985 the Guinness Group took over the Arthur Bell company, including this distillery.

In 1987 a visitors' centre was built to cope with an increasing tourist trade keen to sample the wares.

Blair Athol, after which the malt is named, was the estate village of Blair Castle at whose gates it stands. It is now a popular tourist centre.

Queen Victoria, an inveterate explorer of the Highlands, held many a royal picnic in this area with enough retainers around her to mount a major expedition. Her Royal Highness was fond of the national drink, especially after a day of sight-seeing.

Visiting:
+44 (0) 1796 482003.

Blair Athol Distillery.

Tasting Notes

Ideal after a meal with its warm, relaxing ambience, this mild dram is also delicate with a trace of wood smoke.

Blair Castle.

24

Bowmore

School Street, Bowmore,
Isle of Islay PA43 7JS.

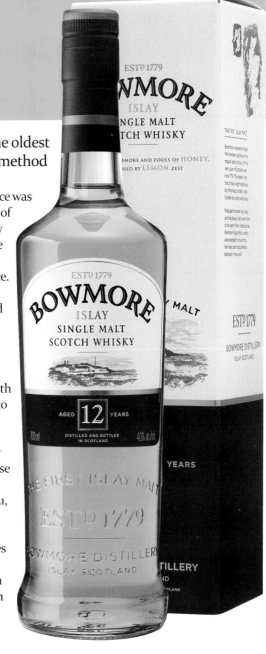

Founded in 1779 on the shore of Loch Indaal, this is one of the oldest distilleries in the Hebrides and retains the traditional floor method of malting barley.

Traditionally each distillery had its own extensive malting floor where produce was regularly turned by teams of experts. They stirred the germinating seed mixture of water, yeast and barley which was then converted into a suitably malted mash by soaking and fermenting for three to five days to produce the final product for the distillation process in whisky making. Nowadays most distilleries use modern, mechanical equipment with automated 'maltsters' to produce their final produce.

Various drinks critics have tried to capture the essence of Bowmore.

Among the many descriptions are: "the pale colour belies the character and flavour that this dram possesses since the peat reek is evident from the first whiff and, although not as pronounced as some of its neighbours, this gives great charm with a palate that is salty sweet as well as possessing a lovely, long and refreshing finish" or "having a gold, pale straw colour, the nose fills with smoky peat, sea salt and iodine thanks to a rich, woody and complex aroma with a long, lingering, malt finish intertwined with more sweet peat, all adding up to an amazing finish!"

The water source for this malt is the Laggan River and two million litres of the spirit are produced annually. It was one of the first legal distilleries on Islay and one of the warehouses was converted into the village swimming pool whose waters were warmed with waste heat from the distillery.

The winner of numerous awards, the best Bowmore vintages are 12, 15, 17, 21, 25, 30 and 40 years old.

Bowmore village itself, where the distillery is based, flourishes as the administrative centre of this Inner Hebridean island where all the main villages sound like a roll call of Scotland's best malts.

Whisky has long been Islay's main export and there is almost something in the air – and certainly in the ground and on the lochs – which makes it such an excellent centre for making whisky.

Visiting: +44 (0) 1496 810671.

Tasting Notes

Long and mellow, this dram has contrasting flavours of peatiness and smoke on the taste buds. An ideal restorative in the dusk of the day.

Bowmore Distillery.

Bowmore Vaults.

Bruichladdich

Isle of Islay PA49 7UN.

This distillery is on the western shore of Loch Indaal on Islay in the Inner Hebrides and went into production in 1881. The name is Gaelic for 'the hill on the shore' and is drawn directly from the heather-covered hills.

The production methods involve a combination of ancient and modern. Master Distiller Jim McEwan, an ex-Bowmore man steeped in whisky folklore and practice, twice Distiller of the Year, has overseen the renaissance of Bruichladdich.

Joining up with other distilling friends and entrepreneurs, he has helped put this venerable island distillery back on the map.

Closed during the Great Depression from 1929 till 1937, it underwent renovations and a pair of new stills were added to the original pair in 1975.

Mothballed again in the last five years of the 20th century, it was bought from owners Whyte and Mackay by a small independent group of private individuals and in May, 2001, the first distillation took place under new management.

After a five-month refurbishment of old, existing machinery, some of which dated back more than a century, a new whisky, based on an original distillation process from the end of the 19th century, was successfully produced.

The owners are fiercely proud of their independent status which has been achieved using mainly Scottish money.

Modern technology is kept at a minimum while tried and tested and time-honoured methods are enshrined which the owners maintain produce the best results, sometimes even to the surprise of experts.

Distillery manager Allan Logan sampling how the distillery's product is progressing.

The cask wood types used to mature the spirit are laid down for full term maturations and nothing is rushed. Barrels include port, Madeira, rum, sherry and bourbon seasoned wood.

The Laddie Ten is one of this distillery's proudest achievements, the number referring to the decade this malt has spent maturing in barrels.

Visiting: +44 (0) 1496 850190.

Bruichladdich Distillery.

Adding a first water to the bere barley mash.

Tasting Notes

A typical Islay malt, this dram's flavour is full of peat smoke and is velvety, glowing and exciting with a golden luminosity in colour.

Bunnahabhain

Port Askaig, Isle of Islay PA46 7RP.

This is most renowned as a twelve-year-old single malt. The distillery is the most northerly on Islay and was opened in 1883 by the Greenlees brothers, local farmers wanting to make use of their excess grain.

The name translates as 'mouth of the river' because the building is situated near the end of the River Margadale which flows into the Sound of Islay.

A road, pier, reading room and schoolroom for children of employees were also built, which gave the site a communal air.

The current owners are Burn Stewart Distillers and they supervise the production of two and a half million litres of spirits annually.

In 1887 this distillery merged with W. Grant and Co. of Glenrothes to form the Highland Distillers Company.

It was mothballed in 1930 due to the global trade depression but reopened seven years later.

In 1963 the distillery expanded and a second pair of stills were added.

This expansion was widespread among whisky companies at this time when the so-called 'affluent society' was beginning after postwar restrictions and the drinks market in general was undergoing a revolution which involved a wide variety of spirits being on offer.

The washback.

Previously unheard-of drinks like vodka and white rum were becoming commonplace in pubs which themselves were being modernized from the old sawdust-floored dens into much more sophisticated places of entertainment.

What would have been frowned on before, namely the taking of women to lounge bars for a whole night's entertainment, now became commonplace and whisky companies had to rise to the challenge.

Like many others, Bunnahabhain did exactly that and brought ancient traditions into a modern setting.

The company was sold to the present owners in 2003 and the malt became a major contributor to Famous Grouse and Black Bottle blends.

Visiting: +44 (0) 1496 840646; or www.bunnahabhain.com

Bunnahabhain Distillery.

Tasting Notes

Darker than the usual malt, this mellow dram has a satin finish and retains a lightness and satisfying springiness in taste, all suffused with a tang of peatiness as befitting a product of the Western Isles.

Maturing nicely.

Caol Ila

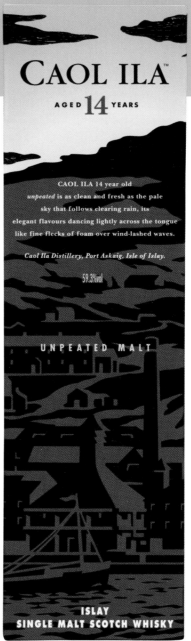

The name means 'Sound of Islay' which is the stretch of water that separates the island from nearby Jura. Lying by the sea, the distillery was founded in 1846 but only reached its full potential ten years later and proved so successful it was widely extended 22 years later when it was largely rebuilt and refurbished with up-to-date equipment.

Drawing water from a nearby fragrant loch surrounded by myrtle and heather, this whisky was also an essential ingredient in the BL Gold Label and Old Rarity blends.

It is currently owned by Diageo and produces a staggering 5,800,000 litres annually.

The flavour is tangy and peaty which is typical of the area.

Like other distilleries on the island, it closed during the Great Depression from 1930 to 1937 when it reopened and was taken over by Scottish Malt Distillers Ltd.

From 1972 till 1974 it was generally reconstructed and re-equipped yet again and its stills increased from three to six.

Like many other distilleries over recent decades it had to strike a happy balance between old traditional methods of production and more modern methods using new technology.

Generally there have been many in the industry who were loathe to even use computers in the making of their products, fearing that this might somehow interfere with the efficacy of the malt whisky involved.

But the most successful have managed the balancing act which involved the greater efficiency of more innovative material with the more tried and trusted ways of production which have lasted centuries.

Visiting: +44 (0) 1496 302760.

Caol Ila Distillery.

Tasting Notes

It is hard to imagine a chocolate taste in whisky but it is there nevertheless, though almost disguised by the tang of damp lawns and bouncy citrus fruits.

The International Wine and Spirits Cup, a contest run by retailers, which has been won by Caol Ila.

Cardhu

Knockando, Aberlour, Banffshire AB38 7RY.

This is best known as a 12-year-old Highland malt. The name in Gaelic means 'black rock' and refers to a feature in the neighbouring Mannoch Hills which are the source of the distillery's spring water.

Set in a remote Speyside glen, it originated when John Cumming took a lease out on Cardow Farm in 1811 and five years later was convicted on three occasions for distilling without a licence.

In fact it was his wife who did the distilling and she used to bamboozle any raiding customs officers by disguising the illicit distilling process through pretending it was all part of her baking for a large family.

Her daughter-in-law inherited the business once it became respectable and extended the property, running things with flair and energy long before feminism became fashionable.

The well-known Kilmarnock-based whisky company Johnny Walker and Sons needed a reliable and worthy base for their blended products and thus bought the Cardhu distillery in 1893.

The current owners are Diageo and they supervise the production of three million litres annually which makes Cardhu the sixth best-selling single malt in the world.

The number of stills were increased from two to four at the start of the 20th century; and in 1902 the Walker family continued to improve and expand the premises with new condensers, steam engines and boilers.

In the third year of the First World War, all malt whisky distillers were closed by government order to conserve stocks of barley.

Thankfully with victory, all the Scottish distilleries were reopened in 1919.

During the Swinging Sixties the Cardhu distillery was refurbished and the number of stills increased from four to six. New equipment meant greater output and a more efficient workforce.

Becoming environmentally friendly long before such a concept was even thought of, coal was no longer used when the stills converted to internal heating by steam from a large, oil fired boiler.

Visiting: +44 (0) 1479 874635.

Cardhu Distillery.

Tasting Notes

This is a malt which does not rely on water to bring out its flavouring which can be as light as a Highland breeze over a field of swaying barley. The taste is clean and rejuvenating.

In days gone by...

Clynelish

Brora, Sutherland KW9 6LR.

Named after a local farm, this distillery was established in 1819 by the Marquess of Stafford who had married the heiress of the vast Sutherland estates and took that name when he was made a duke, becoming infamous during the Highland Clearances for sweeping away 15,000 crofters from half a million of his acres.

The still room.

A huge statue of him still stands atop Ben Bhraggie, which is frequently vandalised.

Due first to the Great Depression and then the war, the distillery was closed but in the 1960s a new adjacent distillery was built and reopened in 1975 as Brora Distillery.

The distillery is owned by Diageo and the water source for the malt is the Clynemilton Burn.

There 4,200,000 litres are produced annually which is one of the highest among Scottish distilleries.

The premises are situated in Sutherland, the most sparsely populated county in Scotland which got its name from being the 'southland' of the Vikings who once ruled here, even though for most Scots it is in fact far to the north.

The landscapes of mountains and moors mean there is plenty of scope for the ingredients of good Scotch whisky to flourish and there are plenty of clear streams flowing down hillsides even if there is a lack of workers to exploit such natural resources.

That's because many of those who could have continued a tradition of making spirits were evicted and shipped abroad by their aristocratic landlords to make way for more lucrative sheep.

Visiting: +44 (0) 1408 623000.

Clynelish Distillery.

Close up of the stills.

Tasting Notes

Dry and cool, this dram retains a rugged flavour of the windswept northern coastline where it is produced and feels robustly individualistic.

Cragganmore
Ballindalloch, Banffshire AB37 9AB.

The current owners are Diageo. The water source is the nearby Craggan Burn and the distillery produces 2,100,000 litres of malt whisky annually. This distillery was founded by John Smith who had a hand in others as well and was the most experienced distiller of his day, having been manager of Macallan and Glenlivet distilleries.

He persuaded his landlord, Sir George Macpherson-Grant, to lease him the land to build a new distillery at Ballindalloch beside the Strathspey railway line in 1869.

The first 'whisky special' train left from Ballindalloch for Aberdeen in 1887 with 25 wagons containing 300 casks of whisky.

In 1917, as the government restricted the supply of barley in wartime, the distillery closed for a year. It reopened when Mary Jane Smith, the widow of family owner Gordon Smith, a descendant of John, who died young, installed electric lighting powered by a petrol driven generator.

This innovation was typical of Mrs Smith who brought a fresh invigoration to the running of the company.

Like others, it was closed during the trade depression of the 1930s and then was restricted by wartime conditions in the early 1940s. It resumed full post-war production with stills that were doubled to four being steam heated from an oil-fired boiler.

Cragganmore single malt is the most complex of Speyside malts and is one of the area's classic brands.

However, the distillery remains one of the smallest and therefore has to operate at full production for seven days a week to keep up with the demand from at home and abroad.

The unique flat topped spirit stills and the traditional wooden condenser tubs promote the malt's complexity.

Visiting: +44 (0) 1479 874715.

Spirit running into the spirit safe.

Tasting Notes

Rich with the tang of wild heather, this malt retains scents of fruits and greenery in general. There is also honey there and chestnuts, almonds and walnuts which inject a raciness into the tasting experience.

Cragganmore Distillery.

The whisky casks in the warehouse.

Craigellachie

Aberlour, Banffshire AB38 9ST.

This distillery is currently owned by John Dewar and Sons. The water source is a spring on Little Conval Hill and the distillery produces 3,700,000 litres annually.

In 1891 the Craigellachie Distillery Company Ltd., a group of merchants and blenders, was formed and seven years later the production of whisky commenced.

In 1916, midway through the First World War when barley production was beginning to be rationed, this distillery was

The distillery staff in 1920.

The mash tun.

bought by Mackie and Co., the producers of White Horse blended whisky.

In 1964 it was reconstructed and stills increased from two to four.

In 2004 the first official bottle of Craigellachie 14-year-old single malt whisky was launched by the present owners.

Like most other distilleries, it saw an increase in production from the 1960s onwards.

Distilling is one of the few industries left in Britain which is capable of a quick and profitable expansion into new markets abroad and even, when good times return, to greater consumption at home.

Visiting: +44 (0) 1340 872971.

Tasting Notes

As fresh as a Highland shower on a newly cut lawn, this malt has a subtle perfume, sweet as sugar and spicy too with a hint of mint.

Craigellachie Distillery.

The washbacks.

Dalmore

Alness, Ross-shire IV17 0UT.

This is a renowned Highland single malt. The first Dalmore whisky ran into oak casks in 1839. Originally there were only two stills but this rose to eight over the years, which produced up to 14,300 gallons of alcohol each week.

The distillery is currently owned by Whyte and Mackay and now produces 3,200,000 litres annually, the source of water being the River Alness.

There is a royal connection with this drink.

In 1263 the ancestor of the Clan Mackenzie saved King Alexander of Scotland from being gored by a stag on a Highland hunting expedition by killing the furious animal with a single arrow shot. The grateful King then granted the chieftain the right to bear a stag's head on his coat of arms along with the motto 'Help the King!'

The Mackenzie family long owned the Dalmore Distillery and every treasured, vintage whisky bottle of The Dalmore is now adorned with a stag's head displaying a dozen points on its antlers thus signifying it is a royal beast.

The Distillery from the shore.

Thus for tasters of this rare brand of whisky there is a reminder of a medieval past allied to all the joys of today.

The distillery flourished and in 1870 Dalmore was the first single malt to be exported to Australia, thus reminding expats of the auld country while giving the colonials a taste of something better than the beer they were used to.

The local fields of ripe barley which flourish on rich, coastal soils are essential in the production of this malt and the fields are even commemorated in the name, Dalmore meaning 'big meadow'.

Visiting: +44 (0) 1349 882362 or www.thedalmore.com

Dalmore Distillery.

Tasting Notes

This Highland malt is renowned as mellow on the tongue with a long and powerfully warming aftertaste.

The warehouse.

Dalwhinnie

Dalwhinnie, Inverness-shire PH19 1AA.

The name means 'meeting place' in Gaelic. This distillery was built at the end of the 19th century where a crossroads for cattle drovers was situated in an area once frequented by whisky smugglers.

The Jacobites were active there during the '45 Rebellion and Bonnie Prince Charlie's Cave is nearby where the fugitive is reputed to have hidden after his defeat at Culloden.

The still room.

This whisky is excellent as an aperitif.

When it was opened in 1897, the product was known at first as Strathspey whisky but the name was soon changed to a more atmospheric description of where it was created.

The brand is currently owned by Diageo who provide two million litres annually.

This distillery was completely refurbished in 1986 and a visitors' centre opened five years later.

Further expansion and renovation took place at the end of last century and the building was temporarily closed, although the casks continued to mature in the dark and silence of the warehouse cellar's storage space.

Dalwhinnie is the highest distillery in Scotland at 1073 feet and its site is suitably shared with a meteorological station.

It is unusual for a distillery to be situated at any height because they are usually down in glens or on coasts where they have easy access to one of the main ingredients – water – as it streams down the hills.

Visiting: +44 (0) 1540 672219.

Dalwhinnie Distillery.

Tasting Notes

A scent of spring pine trees dances through this malt which is also scented with heather and peat, emphasising all the ingredients which make it very Scottish. There is also honey and fruit to stimulate the taste buds.

Close up of whisky casks.

Deanston

near Doune, Perthshire FK16 6AG.

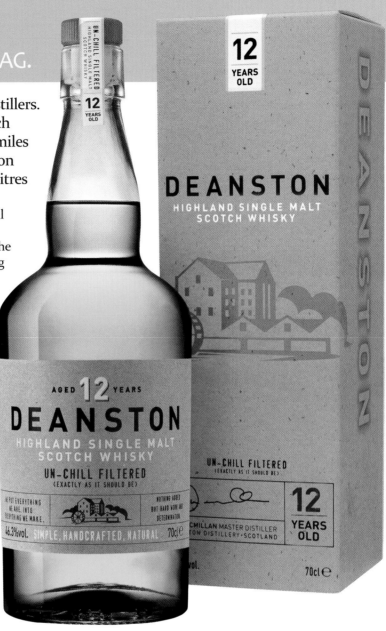

The present owners are Burn Stewart Distillers. The water source is the River Teith which drains the Trossachs lochs and runs 13 miles south east to the Forth. This helps the Deanston distillery to produce more than three million litres of malt whisky annually.

In 1965 what were the buildings of an old cotton mill dating back to 1785 were completely renovated and converted into a working distillery under the name of the Deanston Distillery Co. Ltd, including a former weaving shed that was converted into a vaulted warehouse.

In 1971 the first single malt was released and labeled 'Old Bannockburn', a good Scottish name and the title of the country's most famous battle which was a victory over the English in neighbouring Stirlingshire.

In 1972 the company was purchased by Invergordon Distillers and the first Deanston single malt released the same year.

In 1982 the distillery went 'silent' which is an industry description for production ceasing, usually temporarily. In this case it was for nine years after which Burn Stewart Distillers took over and recommenced production.

In 2002 the C.L. Financial company bought over Burn Stewart and four years later Deanston's 30-year-old malt was released.

In 2012 a new visitors' centre was opened at the distillery where the plant's own turbines create electricity, powered by the River Teith.

Vintage malts are 12, 17 and 30 years old.

Visiting: +44 (0) 1786 843010.

Tasting Notes

Cloves, ginger and honey all put in an appearance in the general flavour of this dram which naturally is heavy with malt. The overall effect is like a herbal tonic which almost makes it seem like a natural medicine.

Deanston Distillery.

The warehouse.

Dufftown

Keith, Banffshire AB55 4BR.

The current owners are Diageo. The source of water is the quaintly named Jock's Well in the Conval Hills and the distillery produces four million litres of malt whisky annually, The Singleton being one of its most popular products.

It was founded as Dufftown-Glenlivet Distillery in 1895.

In 1933 it was bought over by Arthur Bell and Sons Ltd. and became a major contributor to their popular blend.

In 1974 the number of stills was increased from two to four and five years later to six.

Guinness eventually bought over Bell's and in 1997 they merged with Grand Metropolitan to form Diageo.

The warehouse.

The town of Dufftown itself, which lies nine miles away from the distillery, is a thriving tourist centre and was once a model or planned village laid out in 1817 by James Duff, 4th Earl of Fife. And just as Rome was built on seven hills so the town was built between 1823 and 1897 on seven distilleries which are still operational.

The little town remains a busy centre for the whisky-making industry and a landmark on the Speyside Whisky Trail, so beloved of tourists, with its own visitors' centre depicting the area's importance when it comes to the making of major malts.

Visiting: +44 (0) 1340 820224.

Dufftown Distillery.

Tasting Notes

As bold and exhilarating as a Highlander charging into battle, this malt is bracing, warming and encouraging. Its exuberance is spiced with violets. A big, heartening drink with a trace of sherry being left on the tongue as an afterthought.

The spirit safe.

Edradour

Pitlochry, Perthshire PH16 5JP.

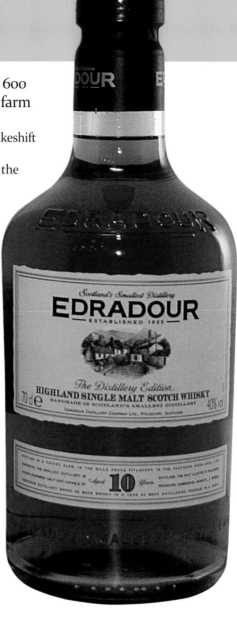

This is Scotland's smallest distillery whose output was once only 600 gallons a week. It is the last of what were numerous Perthshire farm distilleries.

At one time farmers utilized their excess crops in the making of whisky; and makeshift stills varying in size once dotted the countryside.

It was a way of life and viewed as a blessing from God (like a good harvest) until the government took an interest in this lucrative source of tax revenue.

The current owner of Edradour is the Signatory company and the distillery produces 90,000 litres annually, well below the average for Scotch whisky producers but in keeping with this distillery's size and its history of low output.

Nevertheless, the product from Edradour was once viewed as so rare and classy that the distillery traditionally supplied whisky to the House of Lords where it went down extremely well.

The flavour is smooth and malty with a hint of dryness.

The distillery was founded in 1825 by a co-operative of local farmers.

The brand name comes from the Gaelic 'Edred dobhar' meaning 'the stream of King Edred', probably a Pictish chieftain in the Dark Ages or possibly one of those warlike leaders who saw off the invading Roman legions, no doubt after a quaff or two of his favourite malt.

The stream referred to is that which supplies the distillery, namely a spring winding down from the heather-clad peak of Ben Vrackie which towers on the east side of the Pass of Killiecrankie and which at 2,757 feet is frequently snow capped.

The Edradour co-operative became John McGlashan and Co. in 1841.

Working conditions remained frugal and primitive and electricity was only installed at the distillery 106 years later.

It was bought by Pernod Ricard in 1982 and a visitors centre was opened.

In 1986 the company's most celebrated single malt was produced, bottled and disseminated to wide acclaim by whisky connoisseurs.

The company was purchased by Signatory Vintage Scotch Whisky in 2002.

Visiting: +44 (0) 1796 472095.

Edradour Distillery.

Tasting Notes

A velvety, creamy malt with a calm, even finish, this dram radiates gold in the glass and exudes a delicious aroma of sugared almonds with a taste of the sherry casks in which it is matured.

Fettercairn

This whisky is best known as a ten-year-old malt. The distillery was built in 1824 in the rich, rolling farmlands of the north east.

The current owners are Whyte and Mackay who supervise the production of 1,600,000 litres annually.

The source for vital water is the Cairngorm mountain range, a rich and ever replenished fount of burns which water many a distillery in the surrounding foothills.

As complaining locals will always tell you, there is never a shortage of rain or snow to resupply these bounteous streams, whatever the season.

It remains one of the side benefits of Scotland's mercurial climate that there is never any shortage in the ingredients to make whisky.

In 1939 the Fettercairn brand was acquired by the National Distillers of America and in 1966 the number of stills was increased from two to four.

In 1971 the company was acquired by the Tomintoul-Glenlivet Distillery Co. and it was taken over by the present owners in 2001.

This is one of the oldest licensed distilleries in Scotland and produces a fairly rare whisky appreciated by malt aficionados worldwide, being mild and light and not as matured as other brands.

It is excellent as an after dinner refreshment.

Visiting: +44 (0) 1561 340205.

Fettercairn Distillery.

Tasting Notes

Water adds more fragrance to this dram which offers up the zip of citrus fruits and an underlying aroma of burning coals.

Glen Garioch

The current owners of this distillery are Morrison-Bowmore Distillers Ltd. The water sources are springs on Percock Hill and this distillery produces a million litres of malt whisky annually.

It was founded in 1797 which makes it one of the oldest official distilleries in the land. The Glen Garioch Distillery Co. Ltd. was not actually formed until 1908 and in 1943 Scottish Malt Distillers (SMD) took over the running of the business.

Oldmeldrum.

In 1968 it was closed for a couple of years which was out of the ordinary in that it was a generally productive year for whisky making; and then purchased by Stanley P. Morrison, now Morrison-Bowmore Distillers Ltd.

In 1973 the number of stills was increased from two to three and in 1995 it was mothballed for another couple of years before being renovated and reopened.

This distillery's greenhouses are heated by waste heat and carbon dioxide garnered from the on-site distillation process, proving that the industry is well aware of environmental problems in the 21st century.

The best vintages for Glen Garioch are 8, 12, 15 and 21 years old.

There are also various Glen Garioch special cask bottlings, including anniversary ones.

Visiting: +44 (0) 1651 873450.

Tasting Notes

Clean and fresh, this malt nevertheless has a very fruity taste with reminders of melon, pears, peaches and apricots in the mixture, all enhanced by an addition of fresh water.

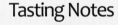

The Glen Garioch Distillery.

Glen Garioch still room.

Glen Grant

Elgin Road, Rothes, Aberlour, Moray AB38 7BS.

This distillery was established in Rothes by brothers James and John Grant who are represented by the two Highlanders on the label gathered round a barrel of their product.

They came from a long line of local farmers whose living had long since been supplemented by the illicit production of malt whisky.

James Grant went on to become a prominent businessman and Provost of Elgin.

This whisky business expanded at the start of the 20th century and was eventually bought over by the Seagram Company of Canada in 1978.

Like many of its ilk, this distillery uses water from a nearby burn – in its case the Glen Grant burn – and its eight large stills are coal fired as of old.

The current owners are Campari of Milan and the distillery produces 5,900,000 litres annually.

This is the only single malt whose label bears the names of its founders.

Glen Grant Victorian Gardens.

Established by John Grant in 1840, by 1961 it had become a worldwide brand and was the bestselling Scotch in Italy, a position it has held to this day.

In 1973 the stills were increased from four to six and when it was bought over by Seagrams four years later the coal fired stills were increased from six to ten.

The firm was purchased by Campari in 2006 who appreciated it was a phenomenon in Italy; and the malt is an important component of Chivas Regal whisky.

The owners take pride in the historic fact that there have only been nine managers in the distillery's history and only four blenders.

The Grant family over the decades were the first to shed electric light on their business and also introduced tall, slender stills and purifiers which created the fresh, malty flavour and clear colour that defines Glen Grant whisky to this day.

It is the only distillery to have its own Victorian garden which includes woodland walks for visitors.

Visiting: +44 (0) 1340 832118 or www.glengrant.com

Dennis Malcolm – Master Distiller.

Glen Grant Distillery.

Tasting Notes

Smooth and delicate with shades of pale amber in colouring, this dram is medium bodied and rich in malt.

Glen Moray

Elgin, Morayshire IV30 1YE.

The current owners of this distillery are La Martiniquaise, who are France's second largest distributor of wines and spirits behind Pernod Ricard. This distillery produces two million litres plus of malt whisky annually, drawing its water from the River Lossie.

It was first established by the Glen Moray - Glenlivet Distillery Co. in 1897 and closed in 1910 before being reopened in the 1920s after being purchased by Macdonald and Muir.

In 1958 the stills were increased from two to four.

The building was converted from a brewery as was its sister distillery at Glenmorangie.

The warehouses are close to a former place of execution for 17th century criminals known as Gallowscrook Hill.

The best vintages are 12 and 16 years old.

Moray or Morayshire (formerly Elginshire), from which this whisky takes its name and within which it is produced, with its rich agricultural landscapes in the north of its 476 square miles, is a county ideal for whisky making, having a rich array of the needed ingredients, especially an abundance of water and crops.

Bounded to the north by the Moray Firth and with Elgin as its county town, Moray is bordered to the east by Banffshire, on the south by Inverness-shire and to the west by Nairnshire, all themselves counties which include distilling as a major local industry.

The south of Moray consists mostly of upland forests so most of the distilling processes take place in the northern half.

Visiting: +44 (0) 1343 550900.

Elgin from Lady Hill.

Tasting Notes

Fiery in taste, this dram is rich with Scottish ingredients like oatmeal, shortbread, blackcurrants and even a lemony grassy flavour. Water as usual helps bring out the tang of heather.

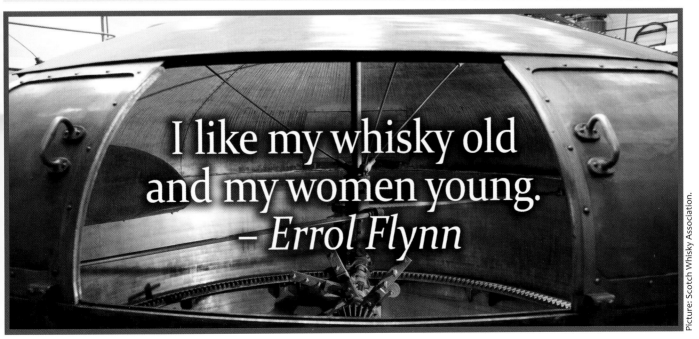
I like my whisky old and my women young. – Errol Flynn

Glen Ord

Muir of Ord, Ross-shire IV6 7UJ.

It was built in 1838, on the site of a smuggler's bothy beside the village of Muir of Ord, eight miles from Inverness. In those days and at that time many illegal whisky-making ploys used to be devised by devious Highlanders. This distillery is the last of many that once flourished in this area. It produces the celebrated Glen Ord 12-year-old single malt whisky and The Singleton single malt, pictured right.

The company is currently owned by Diageo and the source of its water is two local lochs.

There are four million litres of the malt produced annually.

After it was established as the Ord Distillery Company, it went bankrupt nine years later.

In 1878 the jinx continued when a new building was erected only to be later burnt down in a fire.

The business was purchased by John Dewar and Sons in 1923 then Scottish Malt Distillers a few years later.

In 1966 the premises were renovated and expanded to six stills and in 1988 a visitors' centre was opened.

In 2010 another major refurbishment took place.

This whisky contributed extensively to Johnnie Walker blends.

The product has also been marketed in the past with varying success as Glenordie, Ord and Muir of Ord.

Visiting:
+44 (0) 1463 872004.

Glen Ord Distillery.

Tasting Notes

Peppery, this malt is a fine restorative with a flavour full and round, rich and fresh.

The water was not fit to drink. To make it palatable, we had to add whisky. By diligent effort, I learnt to like it.
– Sir Winston Churchhill

Glen Scotia

Campbeltown, Argyll and Bute PA28 6DS.

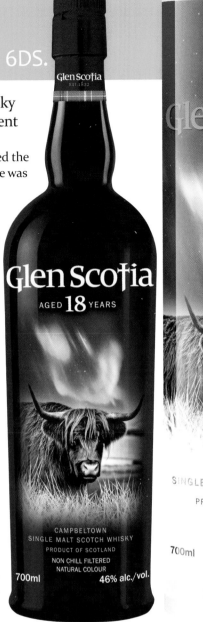

I t's not only the hauntingly rich flavours of this whisky that attract so much attention. An altogether different type of spirit also makes its presence felt.

In 1924 a manager by the name of Duncan MacCallum acquired the distillery from West Highland Malt Distillers Ltd but good fortune was not to last and the plant closed in 1928.

It is claimed that having been swindled out of a huge fortune in 1930, MacCallum drowned himself in the Campbeltown Loch.

To this day people swear they see the disgruntled ghost of this former owner roaming the distillery grounds.

Campbeltown, on the tip of the Kintyre Peninsula, once boasted 34 distilleries, large and small between 1817 and 1880. But there are now just two, Glen Scotia and Springbank.

Like the local area, this plant has also had a bumpy ride since first opening for business in 1832.

In 1919 it was purchased by West Highland Malt Distilleries Ltd. However, for five years from 1928 it was closed before being acquired by Hiram Walker.

In 1970 it became part of Amalgamated Distilled Products Ltd, but was closed in 1984.

In 1989 it was purchased again, this time by Gibson International, who had it for ten years before the operation required more investment.

The distillery was then snatched from receivership by Glen Catrine who put it up for sale where it was purchased by the present owners Loch Lomond Distillery, who have since refitted the premises and recommenced distilling.

They are tasked with producing 750,000 litres of malt whisky annually, drawing water from a private well to supplement their other source at Crosshill Loch.

The best vintages of Glen Scotia are 12, 14, 18 and 26 years old.

Visiting: +44 (0) 1586 552288.

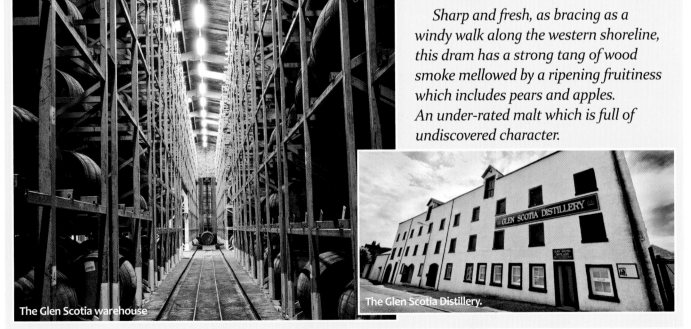

The Glen Scotia warehouse

The Glen Scotia Distillery.

Tasting Notes

Sharp and fresh, as bracing as a windy walk along the western shoreline, this dram has a strong tang of wood smoke mellowed by a ripening fruitiness which includes pears and apples.
An under-rated malt which is full of undiscovered character.

Glenburgie

By Alves, Forres, Morayshire IV36 2QY.

ituated amongst a vast patchwork of farm fields in the far north of Scotland, the view of lush, smoothly undulating countryside stretches out towards an endless horizon.

Started in 1810 it was the area's endless supply of pure fresh water that established the distillery in its location every bit as much as the beauty of the surrounding landscape.

Glenburgie's inconspicuous beginnings are to be found in a modest stone structure which was named Kilnflat until it acquired its present day moniker in 1878.

However it has not been plain sailing from day one.

The plant closed for eight years in the 1870s due to a periodic trade depression, a phenomenon which regularly afflicts the industry but proved not to be as big a drawback in this case as one would imagine.

Unlike in some other businesses distilleries, if kept well in order, could then and still can today reopen comparatively quickly after such events.

Glenburgie Distillery.

The Glenburgie Distillery managed to survive the travails of the Great Depression and stayed open, being operated by Hiram Walker and in 1936 the American grocer who owned Ballantine's at the time eventually decided to buy over the firm.

The water sources are local springs and this distillery produces four million litres of malt whisky annually.

With the natural ingredients for making the coveted liquid product in abundance, especially the all-year-round water supply provided for by the inclement Scottish weather, the distillery has progressed from strength to strength.

Nowadays it is owned by Pernod Ricard and this malt is renowned for its 10 and 15 year old vintages, both produced in good years when the barley crops were particularly rich and ripe and the resulting taste strong and bracing.

One whisky aficionado described Glenburgie thus, 'It is pale gold in colour, big and sweet and malty, rich and full-bodied on the palate with a great sense of balance and intrigue, plus a long, lingering finish with a taste of candied tropical fruit and toffee.' Phew! Who would have thought? One wonders if the old Highlanders would have voiced their verdicts in such opulent tones.

Visiting: +44 (0) 1343 850258.

Glenburgie Distillery Old Customs House.

Tasting Notes

The sherry casks that matured this dram inject a richness to the taste as does a tang of heather. Initially rather dry, it quickly develops into flavours which have a hint of remote woodsmoke about them.

Glenburgie Distillery stills.

Glencadam

Founded in 1825, this distillery passed through a number of owners until purchased by Hiram Walker in 1954. It has two stills and is half a mile from the River Esk, taking its water from springs in the surrounding hills.

The current owners are Angus Dundee plc.

There are 1,500,000 litres produced here annually.

In 1959 the premises were renovated but a few years later the business was mothballed by operators Allied Distillers due to over-production.

This went against the national trend at the time when distilleries were expanding due to the Swinging Sixties which introduced fatter wallets along with more discerning and sophisticated tastes.

However, it was bought by the current owners in 2003 and production resumed.

This whisky was an important component of Stewart's Cream of the Barley blend and also Ballantine's blends.

The best vintages are 10, 12, 14, 15 and 21 years old.

Glencadam still lye pipe.

Visiting: +44 (0) 1356 622217.

Tasting Notes

Floral with traces of oranges and citrus fruits, this malt is elegant, light golden in colour and peppered with a refined dark oak undertow. An aristocrat among drams.

Glencadam Distillery.

Welcome.

GlenDronach

Forgue, Huntly,
Aberdeenshire AB5 6DB.

One of the earliest licensed distilleries in Scotland, its founder, James Allardes, was a frequent guest of the 5th Duke of Gordon who was largely responsible for the Excise Act of 1823.

The distillery, which opened in 1826, straddles the Dronach Burn which handily supplies the cooling water and is situated among tall trees in which rooks nest. They are supposed to bring good luck according to local folklore.

The current owners are the BenRiach Distillery Company and it produces 11,400,000 litres annually.

In 1960 it was purchased by Teachers and the malt whisky became an important element in their blends.

In 1966 the coal fired stills were increased from two to four and ten years later Teachers joined Allied Breweries.

The distillery was mothballed from 2000 to 2002 before being reopened under their present management to great success.

The best vintages are 12, 15, 18 and 21 years old. The malt which has been matured 12 years is labeled Original and the malt matured for 15 years is marketed as Revival.

Visiting: +44 (0) 1466 730202.

Tasting Notes

Spicy, smoky, this malt is airy and rich, full and smooth, with a taste medium to dry.

GlenDronach Distillery in the summer.

GlenDronach stills.

Glenfarclas

Ballindalloch, Speyside AB37 9BD.

This whisky is a single Highland malt whose age can range from eight to 25 years. Run by the Grant dynasty, it was inaugurated in 1836.

The name means 'glen of the green grasslands' in Gaelic and the site was originally a staging post between cattle, horse and sheep farms and the market at Elgin.

It became popular in the USA once Prohibition was repealed.

The water source is streams from nearby Ben Rinnes.

There are three million litres produced annually.

The distillery was reconstructed and modernized at the end of the 19th century and in 1960 the number of stills was increased from two to four.

In 1973 a visitors centre was opened on the site where three years later the number of stills was increased from four to six.

Rolling out the casks.

This distillery contains the largest stills on Speyside and it has been under the same Grant family ownership since 1865.

Like most distilleries in the neighbourhood and further afield, it has seen a gradual increase in production as the market boomed.

Even after home sales reached a peak, there was room for further divergence abroad, first in America and then in Asia and eventually worldwide.

Visiting: +44 (0) 1807 500257.

Tasting Notes

A dark, mysterious malt, the flavour lingers long in the taste buds and is silkily smooth and full bodied.

The Distillery from the barley field.

The still house and spirit safe.

Glenfiddich

Dufftown, Banffshire AB55 4DH.

This spirit prides itself on being the leading Scotch malt whisky and was founded by distiller William Grant who used the power of the Fiddich River winding through the Conval Hills to drive his machinery.

Grant began working on the project in the summer of 1886, aided by his seven sons and two daughters and laboured away by hand.

With the help of just a mason and carpenter, Grant, always frugal, built his distillery using second hand stills for just £700. The first whisky was produced on Christmas Day, 1887, which proved to be a celebratory date in more ways than one.

The product prospered so much that he built a second distillery at nearby Balvenie.

The distillery has remained in the Grant family, being currently owned by William Grant & Sons Ltd., making the firm a rarity – just like the whisky – with regards to longevity amongst the major distillery owners.

The water for the malt is currently supplied by the nearby Robbie Dhu springs and there are ten million litres produced annually which makes it one of the most productive distilleries in Scotland.

In 1961, influential designer Hans Shelger created a triangular bottle for Glenfiddich, which was considered radical at the time.

In 1963 the firm began marketing a single malt to meet demand and in 1991 it first produced 500 bottles of 50-year-old Glenfiddich whisky.

The warehouse.

On site there is a cooperage and coal fired stills and it is the only Highland single malt distillery where the product is distilled, aged and bottled on the premises.

Glenfiddich's 30-year-old whisky won the gold medal at the International Wine and Spirit competition in 2000 when William Grant and Sons Ltd. also won the Distiller of the Year award.

In 2001 the distillery released a 64-year-old single malt, which at the time was the world's oldest. Only 61 bottles survived from the original cask.

Visiting: +44 (0) 1340 820373.

Tasting Notes

Distinctively pale in colour, this malt is fresh, invigorating and dry, smooth as velvet.

The still room.

Glenfiddich Distillery.

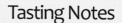

Glengoyne

Dumgoyne near Killearn, Stirlingshire G63 9LB.

The Glengoyne Distillery.

This distillery is in a wooded glen at the foot of Dumgoyne Hill in the Campsie Hills and at one time romanticised cattle rustler Rob Roy was active in the area.

The distillery was founded in 1833 but bought in 1876 by the wine merchants Lang Brothers who changed the name to Glen Guin, extending and modernising the premises.

They changed the name back to its present one in 1908.

In the mid-1960s, in common with similar premises and due to the upturn in trade, the distillery was modernized and reconstructed and the stills increased from two to three.

In 2003 the current owners, Ian Macleod Distillers Ltd. purchased the business.

The water source is the Blairgar Burn which runs down from the Campsies, clear liquid that is famed for its softness.

Like all good malt whiskies the highest-quality barley is soaked in water and spread out on the floor of the malthouse to be turned regularly.

Usually once germination has taken place it is dried using the smoke from peat fires which impart an aromatic flavour to the drying malt.

However, the Glengoyne distillery is different as it uses only barley that has been dried using warm air which gives in the finished product a more subtle chance for flavours to express themselves.

Glengoyne is also used in the blends that make up Famous Grouse and Cutty Sark whiskies.

Visiting: +44 (0) 1360 550254.

Tasting Notes

Medium bodied and dark, this dram is sleek as marble, delicate, mellow and mild.

The Distillery in days gone by.

The Glengoyne stills.

49

Glenkinchie

Pencaitland, East Lothian EH34 5ET.

This distillery, just a dozen miles from Edinburgh, has long been involved in things agricultural. Managers in past years regularly won fat stock prizes at Smithfield and Edinburgh markets, with the beasts flourishing on distillery by-products.

There is a museum of malt whisky production on the premises which includes an enormous scale model of a distillery

The current owners are Diageo and it produces 2,350,000 litres annually, the source of water being reservoirs in the nearby Lammermuir Hills.

The distillery was founded in 1837 by John and George Rate but it was closed in 1853 before being opened again in 1880, trading under the name Glen Kinchie.

In 1914 it was taken over by Scottish Malt Distillers Ltd.

From 1988 the whisky product was bottled as a single malt.

In 1997 a new visitors centre was opened.

This malt was an important contributor to Haig's blends.

The best vintages are 12 and 20 years old.

Parts of the Lowlands, including East Lothian, have had a long and distinguished history of whisky making, discrediting the myth that the golden liquid is only a product of the Highlands.

Most of the Lowland distilleries, in common with those elsewhere, have usually been located at the foot of hill ranges where burns could stream down to feed the process.

Close up of still - contents 30,963 litres.

Visiting: +44 (0) 1875 342012.

Tasting Notes

Spicy and polished, the flavour of this dram is dry and malty.

Glenkinchie Distillery.

The area where whisky is fermented from ground malt.

The Glenlivet

Ballindalloch, Banffshire AB37 9DB.

This is the only whisky allowed to call itself THE Glenlivet for in 1880 the exclusive use of this name was secured by John Gordon Smith after he took legal action against other distillers who had been calling their whisky Glenlivet even though their distilleries were not in the glen.

However, the court also ruled that ten other whisky producers could hyphenate their labels with Glenlivet.

But THE Glenlivet was famous even before it was legalised and King George IV was presented with some by Sir Walter Scott on his state visit to Scotland in 1822, the world famous novelist being the official organiser of the regal jaunt.

The first person to take out a licence for this whisky under the Excise Act of 1823 was George Smith who built the Glenlivet distillery with the encouragement of his landlord, the Duke of Gordon.

The business was officially founded in 1824 and the present distillery building was completed in 1858.

It has remained open almost all that time, even continuing to operate during the Great Depression, which closed many other distilleries. Indeed the only time it was mothballed was during WW2 and that by Government decree.

George's grandfather, John Gow, had changed his name to Smith after fleeing the area when the Jacobite cause he supported was defeated at Culloden.

In 1953 the company merged with Glen Grant and in 1977 it was taken over by Seagram of Canada who then merged The Glenlivet with Chivas Brothers to form the Chivas and Glenlivet Group.

Pernod Ricard took over in 2001.

The water source is the quaintly-named Josie's Well and the distillery produces 10,200,000 litres annually.

Much of that goes into six million bottles of The Glenlivet single malt (the USA's biggest selling malt) and the rest is used for Pernod Ricard's blended whiskies.

The best of The Glenlivet vintages are 12, 15, 18 and 21 years old.

Visiting: +44 (0) 1340 821720.

Tasting Notes

There are a few unusual tastes here, like hazelnuts, vanilla and fresh fruits and the American oak in which this malt is matured gives it a warm, generous character.

The Glenlivet Distillery.

The Glenlivet Master Distiller, Alan Winchester.

Glenmorangie

Tain, Ross-shire IV19 1PZ.

This distillery is situated on the shore of the Dornoch Firth near Tain. The name means 'glen of tranquility' as its television advertising has stressed. The distillery was first officially registered in 1843 by the Matheson Brothers but the site by the old farmhouse of Morangie was infamous for the illicit production of alcohol since the early 18th century.

Water came from springs flowing down the Tarlogie Hills just above the distillery.

The water meanders through sandstone and gives an added bite to the flavour.

Plentiful local barley is also used in the production process.

The swan-necked stills installed in the 1880s are the tallest in the Highlands and ensure that only the purest vapours ascend to the top of the neck columns.

A crucial element of the workforce became known as 'the Sixteen Men of Tain' and were also featured in the firm's advertising. This select group kept the distillery's secrets which were then passed down the generations.

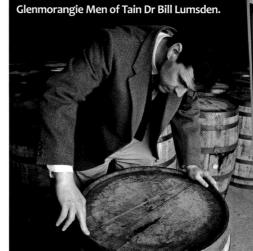

Glenmorangie Men of Tain Dr Bill Lumsden.

This whisky is smoky, delicate, sweet, aromatic and light bodied, being smooth and pale in colour.

It was also a flavour which allowed the *Scotland the What* entertainment trio in their lyrical, melodic paean of praise to Scotch – "These are my Glens" – to rhyme 'morangie' with 'orangey'.

The current owners are Glenmorangie plc and four million litres of malt whisky are produced annually.

The current distillery was completely rebuilt and modernized in 1883.

It was closed from 1931 to 1936 during the Great Depression and again from 1941 to 1944 during the Second World War.

In 1980 the number of stills increased from two to four and a decade later from four to eight which shows the increasing popularity of this particular brand.

The best vintages are 10, 15 and 18 years old.

Visiting: +44 (0) 1862 892477.

Tasting Notes

In keeping with its name, though that is only a coincidence, there is a distinctive tang of oranges in the flavour of this malt and the taller stills help bring out flavours of toffee and peaches.

The Glenmorangie Distillery.

Glenmorangie still house.

Glenrothes

Rothes, Moray AB38 7AA.

The Highland Distillers Co. are the current owners of this distillery. The water sources are springs in the heather-clad hills above the distillery and 5,600,000 litres of malt whisky are produced here annually, making it one of the most productive distilleries in Scotland.

It was founded in 1878 by W. Grant and Co. but merged with the Islay Distillery Co. nine years later to form Highland Distilleries Ltd.

The building was destroyed by a bad fire in 1922 but reopened within months.

In 1963 the stills were increased from 4 to 6 and in 1980 these were then extended to ten which explains the impressive production rate.

Marketed by Berry Brothers and Rudd, this malt, very popular with blenders for decades, is a major contributor to Cutty Sark and Famous Grouse blends.

It is one of five distilleries in Rothes, a small town not immediately connected with whisky making in the public mind.

However, Rothes lies nine miles south east of Elgin, itself a prosperous whisky making area, and is in the 'whisky county' of Moray.

The understated rounded bottle is based on the distillery's classic sample bottle.

The town has also been occasionally flooded by the overflowing River Spey, especially where the Rothes burn flows into it.

Being almost in Banffshire, Rothes is thus deep in Speyside distilling country.

The Glenrothes Distillery.

The stills.

Tasting Notes

As if after sleeping in the silent dark, this whisky welcomes a fresh jolt of water to bring out dramatically its perfumed floral scents of honeysuckle, wildflowers and roses, plus flavours of citrus fruits, newly mown hay and nutmeg. There is also a hint of raisins lingering in the background.

Glenturret

The Hosh, Crieff, Perthshire PH7 4HA.

Situated six miles northwest of the thriving town of Crieff, this is reputed to be the oldest single Highland malt distillery in Scotland. It was officially established in 1775, though the site dates back to 1717 when there were numerous illicit stills in Glenturret, all drawing their water from the Turret burn and loch which gave the area its name.

It ceased distilling in 1921 but James Fairlie bought it in 1957 and began a business revival so that it was producing profitable spirits again three years later.

Touser, the distillery cat (1963 – 1987), was born in the still house and was said to be the greatest mouser ever. She is on record as having disposed of 28,899 mice (though it is not clear who was doing the counting).

This whisky is mellow, full bodied and smooth. It is very light in colour and is usually drunk without water.

The current owners are Highland Distillers and the distillery produces 340,000 litres of malt whisky annually.

In 1981 the company was taken over by Cointreau before continuing under its present owners.

The best vintages are 12, 15, 18, 21 and 25 years old.

This whisky has won numerous gold medals internationally and its success has obviously proved the rejuvenation was well worthwhile.

Visiting:
+44 (0) 1764 656565.

Tasting Notes

There is a balancing note of old oak in this dram which underscores flavours of sweet honey, fresh fruits and barley.

Glenturret bonded warehouse.

Cask filling.

Highland Park

Holm Road, Kirkwall, Orkney KW15 1SU.

This is Scotland's – indeed the world's – most northerly distillery and is sited overlooking Scapa Flow, once the main natural anchorage of the Royal Navy.

Magnus Eunson, an infamous local smuggler, operated an illicit still in the area during the 18th century.

One of his captors, an excise officer by the name of John Robertson, took over the running of the distillery in 1816.

The present building was established in the 1790s making it one of the oldest of its type in Scotland. At one time the workforce did all their own maltings by hand and it remains one of the few distilleries in which traditional floor maltings are still used.

This whisky is smoky, full bodied, aromatic and dry and is best taken with water.

The water sources are plentiful springs that flow below the premises.

There are 2,500,000 litres of whisky produced annually.

It was taken over by Stuart and Mackay in 1876 and they exported the whisky to India which was then part of the British Empire.

Turning the barley.

Another lucrative market lay in nearby Norway which had close connections with the Orkney Islands, the latter once being part of the Viking territories.

In 1898 the stills expanded from two to four.

After various changes of ownership, the Highland Distilleries Company took over in 1935 and in 1999 Highland Park was acquired by the Edrington Group and William Grant & Sons.

The visitors centre opened in 1986 and two years later was awarded Five Star recognition as an attraction.

Visiting: +44 (0) 1856 873107.

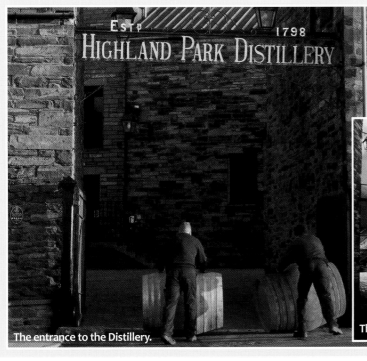

The entrance to the Distillery.

Tasting Notes

Hints of apple, pear and even pineapple soon give way to an enveloping peaty smokiness, plus a heathery, honey sweetness.

The Distillery Office and Shop entrance.

Isle of Jura

Craighouse, Isle of Jura PA60 7XT.

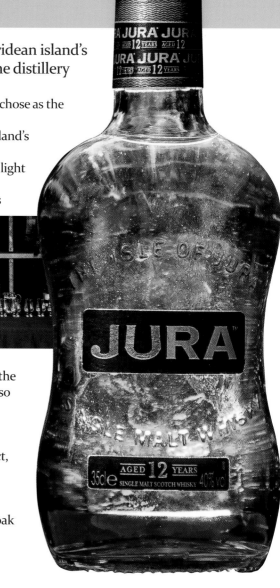

The label of this ten-year-old malt features the Inner Hebridean island's distinctive mountain range known as the Paps of Jura. The distillery opened a new £100,000 visitors centre in May, 2011.

Among the island's claims to fame is that it was the place George Orwell chose as the unlikely spot to write his last book 'Nineteen Eighty Four'.

He apparently enjoyed living a disciplined, spartan lifestyle amidst the island's tranquility.

This whisky is delicate, mellow and smooth with a subtle sweetness. It is light in colour and taste.

The current owners are Whyte and Mackay and the annual production is 2,500,00 litres.

The water source is Market Loch.

The distillery was first built in 1810 but fell into disrepair in the middle of last century. It was completely rebuilt by local estate owners and in 1963 production was increased with the introduction of taller stills that allowed a greater variety of malts to be produced.

Take your pick!

In 1978 the busy stills were increased from two to four.

This distillery's remoteness is part of its attraction and visitors can enjoy the unspoilt scenery, hill walking, climbing and exploring generally. There are also long, empty, golden beaches to traverse.

The distillery sponsors the annual Isle of Jura Fell Race.

Illicit whisky making on the island dates back at least to medieval times.

The soft, peaty water is good for making malt whisky, as you would expect, and the very plain malt, dried using warm air, contributes to the whisky's lighter, softer finish.

The best vintages are 10, 12, 16, 21, 27, 33 and 36 years old.

Casks are important in adding flavour. They are mostly American white oak with some sherry casks as well.

Visiting: +44 (0) 1496 820601.

Isle of Jura Distillery.

Tasting Notes

As befitting an Islay malt, there is a distinct tang of salty sea breezes with flavours of peat and almonds boosting the taste.

The mash tun.

Kilchoman

Rockside Farm, Bruichladdich,
Isle of Islay PA49 7UT.

The current owners of this distillery are the Kilchoman Distillery Co. Ltd. The water sources are local springs and the distillery produces 100,000 litres of malt whisky annually, making it one of the smallest in Scotland.

It is also one of the most modern, having been officially opened in June, 2005, during that year's Islay Whisky Festival; and four years later the first Kilchoman single malt was released.

Kilchoman, pronounced Kilhomen, is a farm distillery and the first of its kind to be built on Islay in 124 years.

The first bottlings were labelled three-year-old but production will be increased vastly over coming years as time progresses and the malt matures.

The fact that it is a small distillery and therefore economic with regards to outlay and overheads may point to future trends.

If demand continues to rise, which it shows every sign of continuing to do, a string of small distilleries throughout the land may be the answer to an expanding industry's necessities rather than the building of ever larger and expensive plants.

This in a way would be a future return to the past because whisky making did not itself begin as a large, money-making business but grew from the roots of the agricultural community over the centuries where individual farms of any size would also have their own stills.

Visiting: +44 (0) 1496 850011.

Tasting Notes

Smokiness concentrated on peaty scents give muscle to this dram. There is also aniseed and citrus fruits in there, all with weathered oak in the background.

The Kilchoman Distillery from the air.

Arriving at the distillery.

Knockando

Aberlour, Banffshire AB38 7RP.

Knockando spirit safe.

Founded by the Knockando-Glenlivet Distillery Company in 1898, it became the first in Speyside to use electricity for lighting. The business initially opened in 1900, but closed within two years. In 1904 it was reopened by London gin-makers W&A Gilbey and much of the make was used in the J&B blend which became increasingly popular in America.

Knockando is Gaelic for 'little black hill' and in the early 1900s had its own station on the Great North of Scotland Railway line which ran east from Grantown-on-Spey.

An individual feature is that its bottle states both the year of distillation and date of bottling. This allows the distillers to vary the length of maturation, which is normally between 12 and 14 years, and facilitates bottling as soon as the whisky reaches its best. This drink is justly celebrated as a twelve-year-old malt.

The business is currently owned by Diageo, which was formed in 1997 when Grand Met merged with Guinness.

The source of water is the nearby Cardnach Spring and the distillery produces 1,300,000 litres annually, although less than a tenth of that is used for single malt. It was renovated in 1969 and the number of stills increased from two to four. Six years later it was taken over by Grand Metropolitan Hotels. Aberlour, on the right bank of the River Spey (a semi-mythical waterway for whisky drinkers) where this distillery is situated, is a small town in west Banffshire, 17 miles south west of Keith.

The River Spey.

Ben Rinnes at 2,755 feet is a local landmark and the area is renowned for its whisky making history, there being 25 distilleries active in Banffshire during the middle of last century.

At a hundred miles in length, the River Spey flows past many of Scotland's most famous brands of whisky and the combination of water and crops produces that unique concoction which makes the best malts so famous worldwide.

Tasting Notes

Aromatic with a hint of nuts leading on to a fruity creaminess leaves behind hints of a lingering toffee experience.

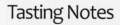

Knockdhu

Knock, By Huntly, Aberdeenshire AB5 5LI.

This distillery is currently owned by Inverhouse Distillers Ltd. The water source is spring water from Knock Hill and 900,000 litres of malt whisky are produced annually.

It was in 1893 that the discovery of several springs of some of the purest, crystal-clear water in Scotland led to the building of the distillery near them.

By the autumn of 1894 construction work was completed and production began in October.

Four years later, due to an increase in demand, additional warehouses had to be built.

In 1930 the company was taken over by Scottish Malt Distillers Ltd. and ten years later there was much celebrating when it was connected to the national grid, previously having survived on its own generator.

Other signs of modernisation came first in 1960 when the distillery's horse and cart were replaced by a tractor; and then in 1966 the furnaces of the two pot stills were converted to mechanical stoking.

In 1983 the distillery was closed for five years before being purchased by Inver House Distillers and reopened.

The product is a major contributor to Haig blends.

The warehouses have retained their traditional earthen floors.

When production first started way back in the 1890s, Knockdhu distillery was held up as a showpiece of its type. The pot stills churned out 2,500 gallons of pure spirit per week, power being supplied by a steam engine.

Cottages were built for the workers and their families, creating a communal atmosphere round the buildings.

Much has been done to update equipment and machinery but the process of distillation has remained basically the same.

Two originally designed pot stills have stayed, giving Knockdhu its distinctive flavour, indeed the same taste as was first sampled centuries ago.

This whisky used to be called Knockdhu after the distillery where it was produced: but the trading name was changed in 1994 to anCnoc, meaning in Gaelic 'the hill', to avoid confusion with Knockando.

Visiting: +44 (0) 1466 771223.

Knockdhu Distillery.

Tasting Notes

Amber in colour with a slight, yellow hue, this malt is sweet and fresh with an appetising fruitiness. It is aromatic with scents of honey and lemon.

The wash house.

Lagavulin
Port Ellen, Isle of Islay PA42 7DZ.

The name means in Gaelic 'the mill in the hollow'. Illicit distilling went on here long before the legal distillery opened. The illegal shenanigans, which date back to the early 18th century, resulted in the formation of at least ten unofficial distilleries on the shoreline of Islay, the so-called 'whisky island' off the west coast of Scotland.

This distillery was the first one to operate legally on the island, one of a pair put up in successive years. It was officially opened in 1816 by John Johnston of a local illegal distilling clan.

The second distillery, constructed by Archibald Campbell, was only worked for ten years when it was considered surplus to needs and demolished. By then both were owned by the Johnston family.

Malt merchant Alexander Graham bought the business from Johnston's descendants after his death for just over £1100. If the price appears low it is because the distillery was in debt to Graham.

Everything connected with Lagavulin is done slowly. The peat is smoked longer, while neither fermentation or distillation is rushed. Maturation is also long—a full 16 years in casks before it is bottled.

The outcome was, and is, a highly-respected 16-year-old malt but it really rose to prominence when it was acquired by Sir Peter Mackie in 1924. He created the world-famous White Horse blend. Lagavulin was its major malt component.

One of Sir Peter's most far-reaching endeavours was ensuring that Lagavulin possesses its own unique fresh water source. That source is the nearby Solan Loch and it helps the distillery produce 2,200,000 litres annually.

Other malts under this brand are 12 and 21 years old.

Lagavulin is smoky, peaty, mellow and full bodied with a lingering taste.

The business is currently owned by Diageo.

In 1962 the premises were entirely renovated and more modern equipment was installed.

The distillery stands beside the picturesque ruins of Dunyvaig Castle near Port Ellen, once the main residence of the Lords of the Isles.

Visiting: +44 (0) 1496 302749.

The Lagavulin Distillery.

Spirit safe at Lagavulin Distillery.

Tasting Notes

Peat smoke is predominant in the taste of this malt but its robust intensity is offset with some traces of sweet fruitiness. A taste of barley soon gives way to a long, warm, peppery finish which leaves the tongue pleasantly stinging.

Laphroaig

Port Ellen, Isle of Islay PA42 7DU.

The name is Gaelic for 'the beautiful hollow by the broad bay'. This distillery was opened in 1815 in a bay sheltered by rocky islands, as the name suggests, and is renowned for producing a unique 10, 18 and 25-year-old range of single malts.

The founders were brothers Donald and Alexander Johnston who were local farmers. They grew barley to feed their cattle and with the leftovers started making their own whisky.

Before long word spread that the whisky being produced at Laphroaig was of exceptional quality and demand grew rapidly.

The brothers Johnston concluded they'd make a better living from whisky than from farming and so they began distilling officially.

Some years later Donald paid £350 to buy his brother's share of the business. However, he died not long after, in 1847, after falling into a vat of partly-made whisky.

As the distillery passed through the generations its fame and popularity grew, especially with other whisky firms who made Laphroaig the most sought-after malt for blending purposes. It's a reputation which exists to this day.

The Johnston family name still appears on the label as a tribute to the pioneers who made its distillation possible.

The current owners are Fortune Brands Inc.

The water comes from the Kilbride Dam and 2,200,000 litres are produced annually.

In 1923 two new stills were added and in 1960 the business was sold to Long John International.

The firm was bought by Allied Domecq in 1990 and taken over by the present owners 15 years later.

Prince Charles visited this distillery in 1994 and handed over a Royal Warrant, being presented with some classic malts in return.

American bourbon casks are used in the maturing process.

Among its claims to fame is that it was allowed to be imported into the USA during the prohibition period because customs officers were led to believe it had medicinal properties!

Visiting: +44 (0) 1496 302418.

Tasting Notes

The sweet nuttiness of barley combines with the pungent, earthy aroma of peat smoke. The heathery sweetness of Islay's clear streams permeate this refreshing dram.

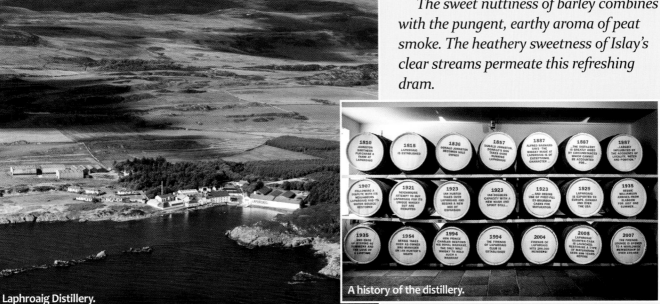

Laphroaig Distillery.

A history of the distillery.

Ledaig

Tobermory, Isle of Mull PA75 6NR.

This is the original name given to the malt now produced as Tobermory by Tobermory Distilleries. The building is the only distillery on Mull and is famous for producing 10-year-old single malts.

The whisky is excellent as an aperitif.

This distillery has had a troubled history since being completed and first going into full production in 1823, 25 years after it was officially proposed.

Tobermory.

It operated under the Ledaig label until closing in 1930 at the first onset of the worldwide trade depression.

It then remained shut until 1972, an unwanted record for a supposedly working distillery.

It traded under the name Ledaig Distillers for a mere three years when the receivers were called in. They eventually sold it in 1978 to the Kirkleavington Property Company of Yorkshire.

The business was then revived ten years later and bought by the present owners, Burn Stewart Distillers, in 1993.

The source of water is a local loch and the distillery now produces a million litres of malt whisky annually.

The Tobermory brand is now only made with unpeated, malted barley but Ledaig is still available in small quantities produced with peated barley.

The whisky flowing from Mull is aged at Burn Stewart's Deanston distillery in Perthshire.

Visiting: +44 (0) 1688 302645.

The Distillery on Mull.

Tasting Notes

Bold yet sweet, this dram has a wide variety of flavours to savour for the discerning drinker, including heather, spices, pepper and even hints of liquorice.

The whisky is aged in Perthshire.

Loch Lomond

Alexandria, Dunbartonshire G83 0TL.

The current owners of this distillery are the Loch Lomond Company. The water sources are bore holes on site and this distillery produces 2,500,000 litres of malt whisky annually.

In 1965 the Littlemill Distillery was established on this site and in 1971 Barton Brands (USA) took over the running of the business.

In 1984 the premises were temporarily closed before Glen Catrine Bonded Warehouses took over three years later and resurrected the plant.

An earlier distillery, also called Loch Lomond from which the present one takes its name, had existed here between 1814 and 1817.

The present distillery is unusual in that due to high efficiency it produces eight different single malts, although only three are currently bottled and sold as single malts, namely Loch Lomond, Old Rosdhu and Inchmurrin, named after the biggest island in the loch, with this whisky's best vintage being ten years old.

There is one still for the production of grain whisky and three sets of malt stills. Vintage malts are for Loch Lomond 23 and 33 years old, for Inchmurrin 10, 28 and 30 years old and for Old Rosdhu 32 years old.

Loch Lomond from Luss.

Tasting Notes

Tang of vanilla and cereals are in this malt along with sharp ginger and peppery flavours which leave a long and refreshing residue on the palate.

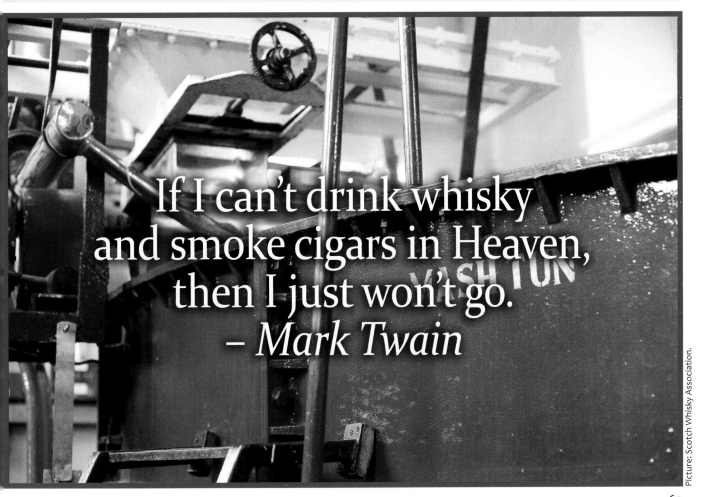

If I can't drink whisky and smoke cigars in Heaven, then I just won't go.
– Mark Twain

Longmorn

Elgin, Moray IV30 3SJ.

The current owners of this distillery are Seagram. The water sources are local streams and the distillery produces 3,500,000 litres annually.

Longmorn Distillery.

It was constructed in 1894 after the Longmorn-Glenlivet company was formed.

In 1970 there was a merger with Glenlivet and Glen Grant distilleries to form Glenlivet Distilleries Ltd.

Between 1972 and 1974 the number of stills was doubled from four to eight; and in 1977 the business was taken over by Seagram of Canada.

A no longer used water wheel and a steam engine are among the historical artefacts on site.

The best vintages are 16 and 33 years old and of the latter one critic wrote: "Longmorn is pale gold in colour, a generous, sweet malt with just a touch of caramel mixed with wood and smoke. Big and more assertively peaty on the palate. Complex, full bodied and classic. It is absolutely scandalous that Longmorn is not known by more whisky lovers. Outstanding!"

Which just goes to show that sophisticated, metropolitan literary appreciations of whisky have come a long way from the days when bearded Highlanders quaffed their latest brew from barley leftovers in small, rudimentary, rainswept bothies up the glens.

Visiting: +44 (0) 1343 554139.

Tasting Notes

Here we are almost in the realms of sweet confectionery with a hint of creaminess spiced with honey, apples and even toffee. Mild in the mouth.

Sample testing the malt.

The controls on the front of the spirit safe.

Macallan

Craigellachie, Banffshire AB38 9RX.

This distillery, built in 1824, lies in the heart of whisky making territory near the River Spey. The product is mellow, full bodied and smooth. According to the James Bond movie, 'Skyfall', the secret agent's favourite tipple is a rare 50-year-old Macallan malt and he was brought up in a Highland glen similar to the ones in which whisky has traditionally been made.

The current owners of Macallan are Edrington and William Grant & Sons. Water is used from local bore holes to help produce six million litres of whisky annually.

In 1892 the buildings, plant, machinery and warehouses were all overhauled and greatly improved. That same year the business came under the ownership of Roderick Kemp, from Elgin.

Easter Elchies House.

When he died in 1909 the Roderick Kemp Trust took over and the Kemp family retained its link with the distillery right up until 1996.

In 1965 the small copper stills (the smallest on Speyside) were increased from six to twelve; and a year later the then owners, Macallan-Glenlivet, went public with their company.

In 1974 the number of stills was increased from 12 to 18 and a year later this was upped to 21, the smaller size needing a greater increase in number due to the increasing popularity of the brand.

In 2000 the firm was acquired by its present owners and in 2001 a new visitors' centre was opened.

Macallan was not bottled as a single malt until the late 1970s but now is recognised worldwide as one of the finest of whiskies, so James Bond was right as usual.

The whisky is only ever matured in ex-sherry casks from Jerez in Spain. So you could say it is a case of the home of sherry coming to the home of whisky.

The rise in production now means there are classic 7, 10, 12, 15, 18, 25 and 30-year-old Macallan malts for the connoisseur to savour.

Visiting: +44 (0) 1340 872280.

Tasting Notes

Toffee, dried fruits and sherry from the casks in which this much celebrated malt is matured combine with tangs of wood smoke to transport the imbiber back to the great Highland outdoors.

The Distillery from the air.

The still room.

MacDuff

Banff, Banffshire AB45 3JT.

This distillery is currently owned by Bacardi. The water source is the Gelly Burn and 2,400,000 litres are produced annually.

It was built in 1962 by a group of enterprising businessmen in anticipation, correct as it turned out, of the affluent society which would increasingly appreciate the quality of malts.

Such was its success that the number of stills were increased from two to four just a few years later.

Still house and spirit safe.

In 1980 Macduff director William Lawson joined the General Beverage Corporation of Luxembourg which handled Martini and Rossi's global business.

In 1992 the present owners took over.

This malt is a major component of William Lawson blends.

Visiting: +44 (0) 1261 812612.

Macduff Distillery under Banff Bridge.

Tasting Notes

One of the new generation of younger malts on the market, the scent and taste is resonant of oranges, caramel, pepper and vanilla with a grainy tang to reassure that this is still very much a wholesome product of Scotland.

MacDuff Distillery.

Miltonduff-Glenlivet

Elgin, Morayshire IV30 3TQ.

This is a fabled product wrapped up in the history, mystery and mythology of the local area. According to one legend, an abbot once sanctified the waters of the Black Burn and from that moment on whisky distilled from it was blessed with a purity which was like none other, and perhaps that explains the reason why it is so highly prized as a key ingredient in top blends.

The firm was among the first officially licensed distilleries in Scotland.

This distillery itself was built in 1824 on the site of an ancient monastery near Pluscarden Priory on the barley-growing plain between Elgin and Forres, so fertile it is often referred to as 'the garden of Scotland'.

Not surprisingly members of the local religious order where not shy of sampling what must have been considered an almost sacred spirit and thus it's of little surprise that the distillery's old mash house, rebuilt in 1824, was once the brewhouse of monks.

The source of water remains the hallowed Black Burn.

In recent times its mystique hasn't worn off despite the distillery being significantly modernized.

In 1936 it was taken over by Hiram Walker and comprehensively refurbished and then expanded some more in 1974. Allied Distillers bought it in 1992 and in 2005 Fortune Brands acquired control before the present owners Pernod Ricard took over.

A total of 5,240,000 litres of whisky are produced each year and the product has been used extensively in Ballantine's blends.

The best vintages are 10 and 15 years old.

Visiting: +44 (0) 1343 547433.

Miltonduff is used in the Ballantine's Blends.

Miltonduff Distillery.

Tasting Notes

Best taken with fresh, clear water, this dram is comfortingly mellow, full bodied and aromatic.

Miltonduff Distillery stills.

67

Oban

This whisky has the distinction of coming in an unusual bottle with a cork closure. Situated in the centre of Oban, looking out to sea and built in 1794, the distillery predated much of the town. Back then Oban was just a small fishing village before being reborn as a tourist centre and gateway to the islands, thanks to the railway revolution which opened up so much of wilderness Scotland during the Victorian era.

The town therefore grew up around the distillery rather than the other way around which was the norm in the Highlands.

The distillery is celebrated for producing the famous Oban Aged 14 Years single malt.

It is currently owned by Diageo and the water source is two lochs in the hills of local Ardchonnel near Loch Awe.

In 1883 the premises were renovated and brought more up to date and by 1923 the distillery was purchased by John Dewar and Sons.

The Distillers Company took control two years later but the distillery was closed from 1931 to 1937 during the Great Depression, in common with many others.

From 1969 until 1972 it was inactive again while a new still house was built.

In 1989 a new visitors' centre was opened which was suitable for the busy tourist trade in this thriving Argyllshire town.

Visiting: +44 (0) 1631 572004.

The still room.

Tasting Notes

Pale straw in colour with golden highlights, a delicate peatiness permeates the taste, emphasising its smoky dryness.

Oban Distillery.

The washbacks.

Old Pulteney

Huddart Street, Wick, Caithness KW1 5BA.

This distillery is currently owned by Inver House Distillers Ltd. The water source is the Loch of Hempriggs and this distillery produces a million litres of malt whisky annually.

It was established in 1826 and is the most northerly distillery on the Scottish mainland.

It stands in the suburbs of Wick, 18 miles south from John O'Groats, at the northern tip of the rugged, windswept coastline.

An unlikely spot for a distillery some might think, except for its proximity to the North Sea which was used to transport whisky by ship south and abroad.

During the herring boom of the 19th century, many of the part-time workers at the distillery were also employed as local fishermen when the sea-going season came around.

Others were coopers whose second job was to make up to eight barrels daily to hold cured herring for export, especially to lucrative markets in Russia and Germany.

The fishing has long gone but the distillery endures and thrives.

The Pulteney malt was used for many years in the making of Ballantine's blends.

This is the only distillery named after a local worthy, namely Sir William Johnstone Pulteney.

There is also now an Old Pulteney Liqueur in which the traditional malt has been mixed with other Highland ingredients to produce a memorable after-dinner refreshment with a beguiling aroma, redolent of the heathery cliffs sloping down to the waves, which also leaves a rich and fruity aftertaste.

Some folk lazily refer just to Pulteney but the correct title of this whisky is always Old Pulteney.

Visiting: +44 (0) 1955 602371.

Pulteney still room.

Tasting Notes

This malt retains a saltiness of the sea air which blows near to where it is produced. It is deep amber in colour with a hint of pink and is dry, medium bodied and smooth with a clean finish.

Pulteney Distillery.

Port Ellen

Port Ellen, Islay PA42 7AJ.

Port Ellen Distillery, founded in 1825, remained highly profitable and productive until the Wall Street Crash in 1929 devastated trade worldwide, including the whisky making one.

The distillery plant closed but the maltings and warehouses continued operating, being rebuilt and refurbished in the mid-1960s with four stills initially heated by mechanical coal stokers but later converted to steam heated coils.

The distillery again closed in 1983 and the bottled produce has now become very collectable. As before, the maltings continued, this time supplying only United Distillers brands Caol Ila,

A view of Port Ellen on the whisky island of Islay, 15 miles off the Argyll coast.

Lagavulin and its own brand of Port Ellen but now the maltings supply the basic ingredient to most of Islay's distilleries, though to their exact and demanding specifications, the malt's automatic production taking place in huge drums that are like massive washing machines.

Tours of the maltings are by special appointment during the Islay Whisky Festival and are only advised for those who are particularly interested in the technicalities of whisky making. A tour is also not recommended for anyone with a fear of heights.

Tasting Notes

A dry finish with a hint of dark, old oak, possibly from the casks that mature this excellent dram, which nevertheless retains a lighthearted almost delicate taste.

Port Ellen Distillery.

The Distillery from the air.

Royal Brackla

Cawdor, Nairnshire IV12 5QY.

The current owners of this distillery are John Dewar and Sons. The water source is the Cawdor Burn and this distillery produces 2,500,000 litres of malt whisky annually.

In 1812 it was established by Captain William Fraser and in 1835 the word royal was added to the distillery name of Brackla, the business having been given the Royal Warrant and permission to use royal in its labeling, the first distillery to be allowed to do so.

An old label.

Royal Brackla Distillery.

In 1898 the Brackla Distillery Company was officially established.

In 1943 in mid-wartime it came into the hands of Scottish Malt Distillers Ltd.

A pot still.

In 1965, during the rising tide of whisky sales brought on by the affluent society, the distillery was renovated and five years later the stills were doubled from two to four.

The vintage age for this malt is ten years old.

The distillery lies next to Macbeth country, most notably the moodily atmospheric medieval Cawdor Castle where Shakespeare set much of his Scottish play.

The Bard of Avon did not mention whisky in his dark drama, however, for the simple reason that it would be a few more centuries before the water of life became a fashionable drink among the social set of south east England.

It was up to poet Robert Burns, Scotland's National Bard, to extol the glories of having a dram in praise to 'John Barleycorn'.

Nairnshire, where Royal Brackla distillery is situated, is blessed with many of the attributes necessary for the production of good malt whisky, most notably a fertile coastal plain and higher hills to the south, all well watered by many a clear stream.

The county town of Nairn was once called by tourists 'the Brighton of the North' and used to be celebrated for its spas, hotels (all of which served Royal Brackla at the bar), golf courses, hill walking, beaches and invigorating winds.

Tasting Notes

Gently stimulating with medium strength spices prodded on by a verdant crispness, this malt is a creamy concoction generated by an invigorating underflow of virile barley.

Two of the four stills.

Royal Brackla Distillery – established 1812.

Royal Lochnagar

Crathie, Ballater, Aberdeenshire AB35 5TB.

The only remaining distillery on Deeside, this was built in 1826 by John Begg on a site overlooking Balmoral Castle and it obtained the Royal Warrant after Begg shrewdly invited Queen Victoria and Prince Albert to view his premises in 1848.

The regal couple were suitably impressed and gave Begg his sorely sought seal of respectability.

Lochnagar is a mountain made famous by Lord Byron who as a child used to holiday nearby and immortalised the peak in a poem later transformed into a song.

The distillery produces a 12-year-old single malt.

Begg went on to develop the whisky industry by using blends which became world famous, often under the advertising slogan 'take a peg of John Begg'.

The distillery is currently owned by Diageo and produces 450,000 litres annually.

The water comes from burns that happily gurgle down the foothills of 'dark' Lochnagar.

Although this distillery was first founded in 1826, a second building which formed the basis of the present one was not built until 1845.

In 1906 the premises were completely renovated and ten years later the distillery was purchased by John Dewar and Sons.

In 1925 it was then acquired by the Distillers Company Ltd. and in 1963 was reconstructed again.

This site was unusual in that it once hosted several whiskies but now only the one brand remains.

The distillery is just south of the River Dee near the main Braemar-Aberdeen road and is at the centre of Royal Deeside and therefore much visited by tourists ever keen to devour royal lore.

Visiting: +44 (0) 1339 742700.

Royal Lochnagar Distillery.

Tasting Notes

Pale with gold highlights, this malt is sweet and full bodied with a clear, refreshing, bracing after effect.

Royal Lochnagar Distillery still room.

Scapa

Scapa Flow, Kirkwall, Orkney KW15 1SE.

The current owners of this distillery are Pernod Ricard. The main water source is the Lingro Burn which helps Scapa to produce a million litres of malt whisky annually. Remarkably, only three men do all the work, with no automation.

Scapa was founded in 1885 by Macfarlane and Townsend, well-known whisky makers from Speyside.

It was closed down during the First World War but reopened in 1919.

In the mid-1930s during the great worldwide trade depression it was closed again, for a couple of years, but in 1941 it was acquired by Bloch Brothers (Distillers) Ltd.

In 1954 it was acquired by Hiram Walker and Sons Ltd., now part of Allied Distillers. Five years later it was entirely rebuilt, but in 1994 it was mothballed.

Ten years later it was refurbished and reopened and in 2009 Scapa was relaunched as a 16-year-old.

This distillery misses out by half a mile on being the most northerly in Scotland which is nearby Highland Park.

With such a small workforce Scapa doesn't have the resources to accept visitors.

Scapa is an instantly recognisable name, particularly to those of a nautical heritage since Scapa Flow used to be the base of the British Home Fleet.

The Flow, at roughly nine square miles, is surrounded by protective islands and leads to the stormy Pentland Firth and thus either to the North Sea or the Atlantic and is an ideal shelter from the gales which plague this area during the dark months.

It was used to hold the captured Imperial German Fleet after the First World War but the interned officers, who nevertheless retained control of their ships, scuttled the lot in 1919.

The Churchill Barriers, man-made, defensive concrete causeways blocking gaps between solid land, were built by Italian prisoners of war after a German U-boat in the second month of the Second World War daringly penetrated defensive nets and sank the 'Royal Oak', the pride of the fleet, which lay at anchor.

Filling the casks by hand.

Rolling out the casks.

Tasting Notes

Like the safe natural harbour from which it takes its name, this malt is like a quiet haven, peaceful and gentle and redolent of peaches, apricots and spices. There is caramel in there and an addition of water even brings out a hint of cocoa.

Speyburn

Rothes, Aberlour, Moray AB38 7AG.

The current owners of this distillery are Inver House Distillers. The water source is the nearby Granty Burn and the distillery produces 2,700 litres of malt whisky annually.

In 1897 the distillery first started production, the buildings having been built from heavy stones retrieved from the River Spey, so that this river was embedded in the very fabric of the premises as well as being a vital factor in the production process.

The still house had not been fitted with windows, doors or heating and whenever blizzards blew down the glens, as happened frequently in wintertime, the workforce had to labour away in overcoats, scarves and gloves, their breath misting in the cold air like distilled spirits.

There were no unions or health and safety checks in those more robust days and the owners had to rely on the dedication and loyalty of the staff, who, presumably, were just glad of the work.

These same owners were keen to have their filled wooden casks with the year 1897 imprinted on them for this was the diamond jubilee year of Queen Victoria. They were keen to celebrate that fact on their product which they managed to do, but not in great numbers because the distillery had just opened.

The first manager, John Smith, held his position for 31 years, a longevity that became common in the industry which was also gradually synonymous with lengthy passages of time. Loyalties and traditions became part of the fabric in the whisky-making process.

In 1962 two stills were converted to internal heating by steam from a coal fired boiler and this was the first distillery to install a steam driven, mechanical malting system.

Visiting: +44 (0) 1340 831213.

The still house.

Tasting Notes

Round and rich with a taste of toffee and a warm, lasting finish, this malt has an edge of sweetness with a peaty aftertaste. It also has a rich, aromatic, lemony fullness.

Speyburn Distillery.

The Granty Burn.

The Speyside

Glen Tromie, Kingussie,
Inverness-shire PH21 1NS.

Memorial Gardens, Kingussie.

This distillery is currently owned by the Speyside Distillers Company. The water source is the nearby River Tromie and it produces 600,000 litres of malt whisky annually.

In 1895 a forerunner of the present building, the Drumguish Distillery, was founded but closed 16 years later.

In 1962, witnessing the increasing popularity of whisky to a new and appreciative generation of consumers, George Christie, a noted Scotch entrepreneur and whisky enthusiast, decided to build a new distillery opposite the location of the old Drumguish plant.

The construction took more than 30 years and used dry stane dyking in its building, a centuries-old method now only practised by a small number of craftsmen.

King's Crest, a 25-year-old blended Scotch, is also concocted and bottled on the premises.

The best of The Speyside's malts are 12 years old and the first complete distillation in the new premises took place in 1990.

The Tromie, the source of water for the Speyside malt, is little more than a stream and scarcely qualifies as a Highland river. It flows a dozen miles northwards through picturesque Glen Tromie before entering the River Spey a mile north east of Kingussie.

However, as a tributary of Scotland's most famous whisky producing river it has more than enough water to keep any number of distilleries going and is daily restocked itself by small burns coming down from the surrounding hills and by regular rainfall. If there is one natural product the Highlands are not short of, it is water.

Visiting: +44 (0) 1540 661060.

Tasting Notes

The malt of the crop-swaying fields comes through strongly, as you would expect from this neck of the woods, with an underscoring of spices and cream, not to mention a dash of caramel and fudge.

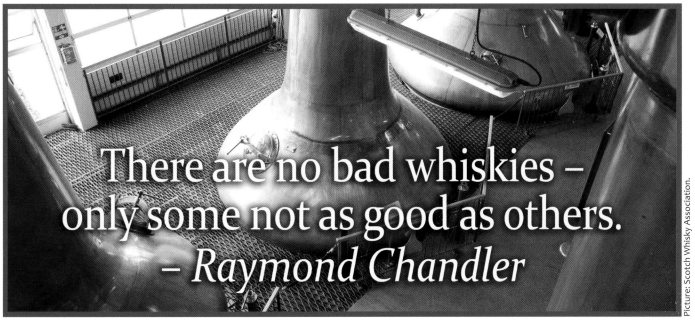

There are no bad whiskies –
only some not as good as others.
– *Raymond Chandler*

Springbank
Campbeltown, Argyll PA28 6EX.

It's not just the care and attention that goes into this produce but also an immense amount of pride. That's what you get when the directors are and always have been descended from the original founders.

Whisky runs through their veins and they have ensured a continuity rarely found in any business, let alone one which is more that 180 years old.

The firm was established in 1828 and nine years later the local Mitchell family took over.

They have ensured that it has stayed under the same ownership ever since, even when the distillery was 'silent' between 1926 and 1935 in common with many others due to a trade slump.

J. and A. Mitchell are proud of the fact they do not chill filters or add artificial colouring to their whisky.

Also it now has three stills, and this means that a portion of the spirit produced is distilled three times.

This distillery is also one of only a few to produce, mature and bottle their whisky on site. They even malt their own barley. The business is thus wholly self sustaining and one that even the greenest of environmentalists would be proud of.

Water is drawn from Crosshill Loch, sharing this source along with the area's other malt Glen Scotia, and this enables the distillery to produce 750,000 litres of malt whisky annually.

The spirit safe.

The plant also bottles a whisky called Longrow, named after a former distillery that once sat opposite the present plant.

The best vintages are many on this ancient brand, being 10, 12, 15, 21, 25, 30, 35, 40, 45 and 50 years old.

Visiting: +44 (0) 1586 552009.

Springbank Distillery.

Tasting Notes

As calmly fragrant as a bowl of fruit salad in springtime, this malt is intermixed with elements of pineapple and passion fruit. All is overlaid with a creamy ripeness which gives the product added power.

Turning the barley.

Strathisla

Keith, Banffshire AB55 5BS.

The current owners of this distillery are Pernod Ricard. The water sources are Broomhill Springs and the output of the distillery is 2,400,000 litres annually.

In 1786 the first plant established here was officially called Milltown Distillery but 84 years later it was changed to Strathisla though in fact it had no connection with any Hebridean island.

The Strathisla Distillery.

Maybe it just sounded more Scottish. Certainly it is now the oldest operating distillery in northern Scotland.

In 1950 it was acquired by Chivas Brothers Ltd., a subsidiary of the Seagram Company of Canada.

In 1965 the number of stills were increased from two to six.

In 1993 Dizzy the cat was officially employed as the plant's 'mouser' among the Bourbon barrels and she was much more efficient than her unfortunate name suggests.

The malt has been a major contributor to Chivas Regal Blended Scotch Whisky.

Visiting:
+44 (0) 1542 783044.

Tasting Notes

A tang of ginger and a hint of vanilla give this malt its distinctive character and there is also a malt flavour to enliven the proceedings.

Sample testing.

The still room.

Talisker

Carbost, Isle of Skye IV47 8SR.

This is the only distillery on Skye and dates from 1833. It lies under Cnoc nan Speirag or Hawk's Hill in a lonely glen on the west coast of the island, a suitably romantic spot, imbued with mists and mysticism, for a whisky-making business.

The business is currently owned by Diageo, although previously it had been in the hands of the Distillers Company who took over in 1925.

The water source is a local burn and there are 2,600,000 litres produced annually.

The premises were extensively rebuilt over a seven year period in the 1880s and further expanded in 1900.

In the early days the whisky was produced using a triple distilling method, but changed to the more conventional double distilling in 1928.

It was reconstructed after a fire in the 1960s which, coincidentally, was a good time for renovations since the whisky-making business was expanding.

This malt has the comparatively rare privilege of being mentioned in literature, appearing in the lines written by Robert Louis Stevenson in 1880 which help make up his poem "A Scotsman's Return From Abroad" –

> "The king of drinks, as I conceive it,
> Talisker, Islay or Glenlivit."

The distillery began producing special bottles for connoisseurs in the early 2000s, with the addition of a 20 and 25 year bottling. Prior to that, only a 10-year-old and an 18-year-old were on the market. The 25-year-old, despite being more expensive than the 20-year bottling, became more popular.

In 2007 Talisker 18-year-old won "Best Single Malt In The World 2007" at the World Whiskies Awards.

Visiting: +44 (0) 1478 614308.

Talisker Distillery from the shore.

Tasting Notes

Peat smoke mixes with sea salt in this malt which also has a warm tang of barley and citrus sweetness ending in a peppery finish.

The Visitor Centre.

Tomatin

Tomatin, Inverness-shire IV13 7YT.

Built where whisky has been distilled for centuries, this distillery was officially opened in 1897. Nearby is the Hill of Parting, so called because it is where the Jacobite clans dispersed after their defeat at Culloden.

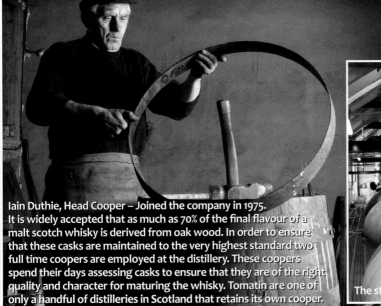

Tomatin Distillery.

It is one of the highest distilleries and was the first to be owned by a Japanese company.

The name in Gaelic means 'the hill of bushes'.

The current owners, who have been in charge since the 1980s, are the Takara Shuzo and Okura company and the water source is All-na-Frithe, a local burn.

With typical Far East efficiency quotas, the building produces five million litres annually, making it the largest malt distillery in Scotland.

It is increasingly popular in the widespread use of blending and the best vintages are 10, 12 and 30 years old.

Established in 1897 by the Tomatin-Spey District Distillery Company, it went into liquidation nine years later but was revived by the New Tomatin Distillers Company in 1909.

In 1956, anticipating the affluent society before it actually materialised, the stills here were increased from two to four and two years later from four to six.

Three years after that they were increased to ten and one more still was added in 1962.

Ten years after that the number of stills was increased to a grand total of 23.

Visiting: +44 (0) 1463 248148.

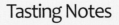

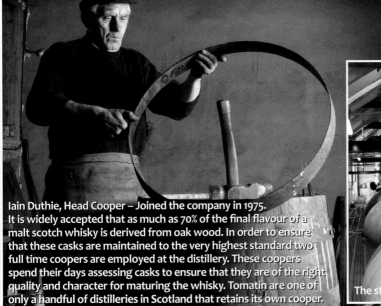

Iain Duthie, Head Cooper – Joined the company in 1975.
It is widely accepted that as much as 70% of the final flavour of a malt scotch whisky is derived from oak wood. In order to ensure that these casks are maintained to the very highest standard two full time coopers are employed at the distillery. These coopers spend their days assessing casks to ensure that they are of the right quality and character for maturing the whisky. Tomatin are one of only a handful of distilleries in Scotland that retains its own cooper.

Tasting Notes

A slightly smoky, peaty flavour gives an edge to this malt's delicate, light bodied taste.

The still room.

79

Tomintoul

Ballindalloch, Banffshire AB37 9AQ.

This is a very modern distillery by the standards of the industry, only being opened in 1965, with the liquid product first appearing in bottle form seven years later.

Built in the highest village in the Highlands, it is frequently cut off by snow in winter, the village always being the first to be mentioned in weather reports whenever blizzards are swirling around the north.

The premises are so extensive that there is local warehousing for ten million litres of malt within the grounds.

The current owners are Angus Dundee plc.

The water source is the local Ballantruan Spring and the current output is three million litres of spirits annually.

In 1974 the number of stills was increased from two to four.

In 2000 it was purchased by the present owners after changing hands several times.

Traditional techniques and natural ingredients at Tomintoul Distillery.

This malt is a valuable contributor to Whyte and Mackay's blends.

The best vintages are 10, 12, 14 and 16 years old.

Visiting: +44 (0) 1807 590274.

The Distillery from the air.

Tasting Notes

Lingering, light bodied and smooth and an ideal after dinner, relaxing dram.

Maturing nicely.

Tormore

Advie, Grantown-on-Spey,
Morayshire PH26 3LR.

A bove the cooperage a chiming clock strikes on the hour with the tune of 'Highland Laddie' and freshwater pearl mussels, that can only survive in the purest water, thrive in the River Spey just below the distillery.

This is not the only impressive sight that greets visitors.

Blending means putting different things together that complement each other to achieve a greater whole – and when done right is sublime.

Keeping with this theme, the way this plant has been put together works every bit as successfully as the whisky it produces.

This distillery was designed by a top architect to blend into the scenery and came on stream in 1959, being the only distillery built on Speyside in the last century.

In 1972 the number of stills was increased from four to eight.

The workers' houses, complete with curling pond and imitation water mill, were specially designed as part of the overall plan to merge with the background. It was environmentally friendly long before that concept became fashionable.

Not surprisingly the nearby small market town of Grantown-on-Spey has become a holiday hub for tourists wanting to explore the Highlands and no doubt the local taverns where the Tormore malt is an additional attraction to roaring fires and good, welcoming company.

What visitors are introduced to is a smooth, delicate, dry drink made with water coming from the nearby Achvochkie Burn.

The construction was financed by Long John Distillers and the business is currently owned by Pernod Ricard.

This malt is a major contributor to Long John blends.

Visiting: +44 (0) 1807 510244.

The Tormore Distillery.

Tasting Notes

An even silkiness characterises this dram along with an exotic trace of melons. Very relaxing after a hard day.

The Tormore Distillery stills.

Tullibardine

Blackford, Perthshire PH4 1QG.

O n the site of an ancient brewery, this distillery was built in 1949 at the foot of the Ochils on the Highland Line where the misty mountains meet the green lowlands.

It takes its name from the nearby moor which is also the location of the Gleneagles Hotel golf complex.

The area has always been famed for the purity of its water which comes straight off the hills in many burns.

The current owners are Tullibardine Ltd. and the water source is the nearby Danny Burn.

Two million litres of whisky are produced annually.

In 1971 it was acquired by Invergordon Distillers and in 1973 the distillery was extended with another pair of stills added to the original two.

In 1993 it was taken over by Whyte and Mackay and in 1995 it was mothballed for eight years before being purchased by the present independent owners.

The warehouse.

The whole area around Tullibardine village was celebrated for its breweries as far back as medieval times and in 1488 one produced ale specially for the coronation of King James IV at nearby Scone Palace.

The architect of Tullibardine Distillery, Delme Evans, also designed those of Jura and Glenallachie.

The best vintages are 10, 20, 25 and 30 years old.

Visiting: +44 (0) 1764 682252.

Tasting Notes

A dry, peppery flavour dominates this malt's soft, earthy taste.

Tullibardine Distillery.

The still room.

All in the Blend

Malts in the following pages are featured in world famous blended whiskies. These include the Famous Grouse, Johnnie Walker, Black and White and J and B.

Allt A' Bhainne

Glenrinnes, Banffshire AB55 4DI.

The name 'Allt A'Bhainne' means 'burn of milk' in Gaelic and for those in the know it really is the creme de la creme'. A relatively new addition to the landscape, the distillery was built in 1975 by North Americans and acquires its water from the springs of the Curran and Rowantree burns producing four million litres of malt whisky annually for Chivas Regal's and 100 Pipers blends.

Although this modern distillery may not be too long established its associations run deep as can be seen for instance in the name, '100 Pipers' which alludes to the 100 pipers who marched with Bonnie Prince Charlie into battle.

This is the fourth Scottish distillery built by Canadian giants Seagrams, a welcome input from a foreign investor and no doubt an equally welcome fact to the army of malt connoisseurs across the 'pond' ready to imbibe the treasures of 'the auld country'.

Currently owned by Pernod Ricard its fortunes have fluctuated almost as much as the ebb and flow of the pristine waters it draws on.

In 1989 the distillery was extended due to an upsurge in demand but then mothballed in 2002 before being reopened three years later.

This chequered career might normally mean an uncertain

We never sleep.

progress in other industries but not for Allt A' Bhainne.

Distilleries like this one can be closed for a considerable time without any damage being done to the site, the business or the traditional product and depends on trading conditions and the amount of produce on the market.

Like all aspects of the whisky making process, the length of time involved in its production is a necessity rather than a drawback and even during the plant's temporary closure the merchandise quietly matured until it reached full fruition giving new meaning to the old adage 'we never sleep'.

The high level of interest for the finished product is such that while not usually bottled as a single malt nevertheless there are occasional independent bottlings available.

Benrinnes

Aberlour, Banffshire AB38 9NN.

The current owners are Diageo. The water source is the nearby Scurran and Rowantree Burns and the distillery produces 2,600,000 litres of malt annually.

This distillery was first established in 1826 but three years later was partially washed away in a great flood which was a judgement and a warning about the sinfulness of his parish, according to the local hellfire minister.

However, a mere natural disaster was not enough to quell the thirsts of discerning whisky drinkers and six years later the current distillery was built on the ruins of the old one and this time there was no judgement on it, divine or otherwise.

It was established by William Smith and in 1922 was acquired by John Dewar and Sons Ltd.

In 1925 it became part of the Distillers Company Ltd. (DCL) and five years later it was taken over by Scottish Malt Distillers Ltd.

In 1955 the premises were entirely renovated, the floor

Benrinnes Distillery in 1934.

maltings replaced and 11 years later the number of stills increased from 3 to 6.

In 1991 the distillery first released Benrinnes as a single malt whisky, employing a rare triple distillation process.

This malt was a long time contributor to Crawford's blended whiskies and was best known for its 15 year vintage. ▶

Dailuaine
Aberlour, Banffshire AB38 7RE.

Dailuaine Distillery.

Probably the Scotch which is most difficult to pronounce – and that is saying something considering all the Gaelic brands in the industry – Dailuaine (pronounced dale-YOU-an) is currently owned by Diageo.

The water source is the nearby Bailliemullich Burn and there are 3,200,000 litres of malt whisky produced annually at the distillery. It was built in 1852 by William McKenzie whose widow later leased the premises to a new company also run by the McKenzie family.

In 1884 the building was reconstructed to become one of the biggest of its kind in the Highlands and five years later the first pagoda roof in the land was added to its splendid facade.

In 1891 Dailuaine-Glenlivet Distillery Ltd. was founded and in 1898 there was a partnership reorganisation after a merger with Talisker Distillery Ltd. based on Skye.

There was a bad fire at the Dailuaine distillery in 1917 which nevertheless did not matter as much as it might have done with regards to production since there had already been a rundown for months due to wartime restrictions on barley usage.

The ruins were rebuilt and the plant reopened in 1920, restrictions on whisky output in general having been lifted a year earlier and this distillery became part of DCL in 1925.

There was another fire in 1959 after which the distillery was rebuilt yet again and the stills expanded from four to six in anticipation of increasing demand.

In 1991 the first official Dailuaine single malt was released as a 16-year-old vintage.

This malt is one of the main components of the Johnnie Walker blend which, under the guidance of owners Diageo, has become increasingly popular in China with Johnnie Walker House now an imposing landmark in Beijing and a magnet for the promotion and selling of other whiskies as well.

Glen Elgin
Longmorn, Elgin, Morayshire IV30 3SL.

The current owners are Diageo. The water sources are the springs from Millbuies Loch; and this distillery produces 1,800,000 litres of malt whisky annually.

Built in 1898 by William Simpson, an ex-manager of Glenfarclas Distillery (and therefore an expert) and his business partner James Carle, full production did not commence until 1900, an auspicious year with the whole of the 20th century before them.

It was then purchased by the specially formed Glen Elgin – Glenlivet Distillery Co. Ltd. in 1901 and was taken over by John J. Blanche, a Glasgow whisky trader, in 1907.

In 1930 it was bought by Scottish Malt Distillers Ltd.

In 1964 the distillery was reconstructed and the stills increased from two to six.

In 1984 it was refurbished again and another new still was installed to cope with increasing demand.

The most renowned vintage is 12 years old. Glen Elgin is one of the major contributors to the making of White Horse

Glen Elgin Distillery in 1935.

blended whisky (named after an old Edinburgh coaching house) which is still popular and owned by Diageo.

The town of Elgin itself, after which the brand is named and where its production point is based, has not been renowned as a whisky-making area but nevertheless remains a busy administrative centre and transport hub for Moray.

It also has a rich heritage dating back to medieval times when the self styled Wolf of Badenoch (Alexander Stewart) burned down the celebrated Cathedral whose ruins can still be viewed. They atmospherically give credence to its once ecclesiastic title of 'the Lantern of the North.' There was always more than one spirit on the go in Elgin.

Glen Spey

Rothes, Aberlour AB38 7AT.

Glen Spey Distillery in 1909.

This distillery is currently owned by Diageo. The water source is the quaintly named Doonie Burn and 1,400,000 litres of malt whisky are produced here annually.

Founded by James Stuart and Co. in the early 1880s, this distillery was acquired by W. and A. Gilbey in 1887.

In 1970 it was renovated and extended by adding another pair of stills and was then taken over two years later by Grand Metropolitan who later merged with the current owners.

This malt is a major contributor to the J. and B. blend.

The best vintages are 8 and 14 years old.

The word Spey in the brand name instantly denotes malt whisky but the actual title Glen Spey is more an evocation than a geographical location since there are various stretches along this celebrated river which would qualify for this title.

Quite why the Spey itself should be so conducive to whisky-making remains a mystery, but one which has been lucrative for many along its banks for centuries.

The river is remarkable for its beauty and crystal clear water streaming over coloured pebbles but otherwise has much in common with other Highland rivers.

It rises 1,500 ft. up in Corrieyairack Forest and, after passing through Loch Spey, flows through the counties of Inverness, Moray and Banff.

In a long descent to the sea – 107 miles in all – it flows through a picturesque strath or vale in the countryside which colloquially could be called a glen. No doubt such tautological niceties are irrelevant to connoisseurs who just like appreciating the qualities of Glen Spey whisky whether such a place actually exists in reality or not.

Glenallachie

Aberlour-on-Spey,
Banffshire AB38 9LR.

Nestling at the foot of 2,756 ft. high Ben Rinnes, this modern distillery is five miles south west of Dufftown in west Banffshire deep in the throbbing heart of whisky making country.

Like many others in the area, it takes full advantage of the streams coming down from the higher land, all of which seem to have some mystical ingredient undetectable by scientific probing, a quality honoured and respected from the time of the Druids (who may have used spirits in their religious rituals) and even before.

The flavour is full bodied, lightly peated and slightly sweet; and it is celebrated as one of the best Speyside malts (not that there are any bad ones).

This is a fairly recent production point (in whisky making terms anyway) since it was only built in 1967 by Mackinlay McPherson Ltd. which was part of Scottish and Newcastle Breweries.

Like others, it was created to supply the demand from the so-called 'affluent society' beginning to flourish at the time and keen to sample the best in alcoholic beverages.

The current owners are Campbell Distillers and they supervise the production of 2,800,000 litres annually.

In 1985 this distillery was taken over by Invergordon and it was then closed for two years for refurbishment before reopening under the new and present management.

The distillery currently contributes to Mackinlay blends and is best known for its 12-year-old single malt.

▶

Glendullan

Dufftown, Banffshire AB55 4DJ.

This distillery is currently owned by Diageo. The water sources are the Conval Hill springs and there are 3,700,000 litres of malt whisky produced annually.

The distillery was first established in 1897 and in 1926 was acquired by DCL.

Four years later Scottish Malt Distilleries took control.

In 1962 the building was renovated and ten years later another adjacent distillery was built to boost production.

In 1985 the original distillery was mothballed and all output transferred to the new plant.

Glendullan was said to be the favourite tipple of King Edward VII, a great lover and imbiber of whiskies in general.

This was the seventh and final distillery to be built in 19th century Dufftown.

It was a contributor to Old Par Blends and the best vintages remain 8 and 12 years old.

Glendullan Distillery.

Glenlossie

Elgin, Morayshire IV30 3SS.

The current owners are Diageo. The water source is the local Bardon Burn and this distillery produces 1,800,000 litres of malt whisky annually.

In 1919 Scottish Malt Distillers Ltd. took over and in 1962 the number of stills were increased from four to six.

This malt is a major contributor to Haig's blends. However, a 10-year-old single malt was launched in 1990 and is still available.

The most famous member of the Haig whisky making family was Field Marshall Douglas Haig who some claim won the First World War for Britain on the Western Front.

When he first came to prominence in the military there was much snobbery and looking down their noses at him from the English aristocracy with whom he mingled and who viewed him as coming from trade and not family breeding. However, his success on the battlefield helped make not just him but also the whisky manufacturing business in general much more respectable and indeed honoured.

Glenlossie Distillery in the early 1900s.

It was founded by John Duff and Co. in 1876. Duff was a well-known character in the whisky world at the time and his enterprise was supported by a number of his friends.

The business was officially formed into the Glenlossie-Glenlivet Distillery Co. Ltd. in 1895. The following year the distillery was rebuilt and modernised.

The taking of large quantities of spirits daily in the trenches and by the military in general, from foot soldiers to the top, is an aspect of that war which historians have somehow never tackled seriously. It was not so much a case of Dutch courage as Scotch courage.

The Haig name lives on in whisky blends with the likes of Haig Dimple and Haig Gold Label remaining popular.

86

Glentauchers

Mulben, Keith, Banffshire AB55 6YL.

The Glentauchers Distillery.

The current owners of this distillery are Allied Distillers. The water source is a dam fed by the Rosarie Burn and this distillery produces 3,400,000 litres of malt whisky annually.

Established in 1898 by the Glentauchers Distillery Co., it associated its name with Glenlivet in 1903 and three years later was acquired by James Buchan and Co.

In 1925 it became part of Distillers Company Ltd. (DCL)

and five years later was taken over by Scottish Malt Distillers Ltd.

In the mid-1960s the stills were extended from two to six and in 1989 it was purchased by the present owners.

The majority of production is used for blending and it is a major contributor, as it has been for decades, to Black and White blends.

However, Glentauchers 15-year-old malt is a much prized possession.

Keith, the second biggest town in Banffshire where the Glentauchers distillery is located, has a justifiable reputation for whisky making, being the fulcrum community for several surrounding distilleries.

The town, that dates back to medieval times, is also renowned as the birthplace of St John Ogilvie, Scotland's only post Reformation saint who was canonised in 1976 and who lived from 1579 till 1615 when he was hanged in Edinburgh and later declared a martyr of the counter-Reformation.

Ogilvie, a Jesuit, was a son of the local landed family who owned Milton Castle in Keith but his opinion of the neighbourhood malts are not recorded, though it is well known that a spiritual bent did not stop holy men from enjoying a dram or two, no doubt on the basis that the Biblical miracle of changing water into wine made alcohol acceptable by the devout.

Inchgower

Buckie, Banffshire AB56 5AB.

The current owners of this distillery are Diageo. The water sources are springs in the nearby Menduff Hills and 2,200,000 litres of malt whisky are produced annually.

It was built in 1871 but the business was liquidated in 1903.

The premises then remained closed but virtually intact, if a bit dilapidated, for the next 33 years.

It was then taken over by the local town council in an attempt to create work during the Great Depression.

The distillery was successfully reopened and proved so lucrative in comparison to past travails that it was bought over by the popular blenders Arthur Bell and Sons and the malt produced became a vital ingredient in that firm's revival in the blended whisky market.

In 1966 the number of stills was increased from two to four.

The most readily available vintage is Inchgower's 14-year-old malt.

Buckie, where the Inchgower distillery is based, used to be better known for its fishing fleet when its skippers gained an enviable reputation for expertise and initiative, not to mention bravery when it came to facing the various moods of the North Sea.

The coming of railways to the north east of Scotland, including Buckie, in the 1880s certainly helped the marketing of local industries like distilling and created conditions for its eventual massive expansion.

Inchgower Distillery in the 1950s.

Linkwood
Elgin, Moray IV30 3RD.

Linkwood Distillery in the 1950s.

number of stills was raised from two to six.

In 1985 the older side of the building was closed but five years later used for production a few months per year.

At one time the then manager, Roderick Mackenzie, was such a cautious perfectionist when it came to running his business that he even forbade the removal of spiders' webs from the premises just in case it affected the quality of the product.

Needless to say, the webs accumulated over the years, much to the discomfort of the workers who fortunately did not suffer from arachnaphobia. They were only removed when Mackenzie retired.

The best vintages of Linkwood are 17 and 26 years old.

The perfectionism of Mackenzie was typical of managers in the business throughout the centuries. Since secretly they did not actually know at the end of the day how their product contrived to manufacture such magic, they did all in their power to maintain 'the old ways' as much as possible to ensure the whisky remained as good as ever.

The industry is renowned for the care taken in production. Even the very word distilling, which comes from an old Arabic expression dating back to Crusader times, meant purifying to perfection which indeed is what each distiller seeks to do.

The current owners of this distillery are Diageo. The water sources are springs near Millbuies Loch.

The distillery was established in 1821 and was rebuilt 50 years later. In 1897 the Linkwood-Glenlivet company was founded; and in 1933 Scottish Malt Distillers took over.

In 1962 the buildings were renovated and in 1971 the

Mannochmore
Elgin, Moray IV30 3SS.

This distillery is currently owned by Diageo. The water source is Bardon Burn and the distillery produces 1,300,000 litres of malt whisky annually.

Built by John Haig and Co. in 1971, it was orginally planned to contribute to Haig's blends.

It was mothballed in 1985 but reopened in 1989.

Mannochmore became available as a single malt in 1992 and the release of Loch Dhu single malt took place in 1986 (Loch Dhu originally meant Black Lake in Gaelic).

The best vintages are 12 and 22 years old.

This whisky is a modern example of an ancient experimentation process whereby malts were mixed together to form blends which it was believed at the start of the 20th century would be more acceptable to the palate of a discerning clientele.

Also, among all classes it was argued that the smoother the blend the more popular the brand.

Distilling is a unique industry in that the building actually turning out the product can lie mothballed for years, even decades, yet the whisky can still be on sale because it has already been concocted years ago and in silent darkness has been simply lying in storage in barrels waiting to be opened and bottled.

The Distillery.

Mortlach
Dufftown, Keith, Banffshire AB55 4AQ.

The current owners of this distillery are Diageo. The water sources are springs in the Conval Hills and it produces 3,800,000 litres annually.

It was established in 1823 by three local businessmen.

In 1852 the distillery was restarted after a few idle years and five years later the number of stills was increased from three to six.

In 1923 it was sold to John Walker and Sons Ltd. and in 1925 the Distiller Company Ltd. (DCL) took over with Scottish Malt Distillers running the business five years later.

In 1963 the distillery was completely rebuilt, one of many that underwent modernisation during that decade of commercial expansion.

It was the first of Dufftown's seven distilleries to be licensed.

The best vintages are 16 and 22 years old.

This malt was an important contributor to Johnnie Walker blends.

The orginal Johnnie, who died in 1857, was a shrewd grocer who marketed his own whisky in his Kilmarnock shop but it was actually his son and grandson, both called Alexander, who expanded the firm and made it a popular brand worldwide.

The first whisky was called Walker's Old Highland blend and the firm's characteristic square bottle was introduced in 1870 which meant less glass broken and more bottles filling the same space.

An instantly recognisable advertising slogan and illustration (at least to an older generation) – 'Born 1820 – Still Going Strong!' captioning a striding Regency dandy complete with top hat, red tail coat, white breeches and dark boots a la Beau Brummel – was meant to represent the canny founder of the firm but in fact had nothing in common with that douce Ayrshire tradesman.

However, it is true the blend is still going strong, for Johnnie Walker House has been opened in central Beijing by Diageo where it is a local landmark and a magnet for those wishing to penetrate the Chinese market.

Roseisle
nr Elgin, Moray IV30 5YP.

This was Scotland's first new major whisky distillery for 30 years and is still being developed by the owners, Diageo.

It has a capacity of ten million litres annually which is double its nearest rival.

In 2007 the first announcement was made by Diageo that they planned to build a £40 million distillery.

In 2009 the first test productions went ahead using local streams.

The company are trying to make production carbon neutral in keeping with modern environmental demands and to this end have introduced many ultra-modern features, including a £14 million biomass plant.

In October, 2010, the premises were formally opened by Diageo's Chief Executive Paul Walsh.

There have been no bottlings as yet but it is hoped to launch a new single malt soon, though as in all procedures connected with distilling such things cannot be rushed.

It is a question of successfully mixing the old with the new and it is good to see such expansion in an era of retraction and austerity. Hopefully it will not be the last distillery to be built this century.

Certainly the international demand is increasingly there to be slaked, while one of the main ingredients – water – shows no sign of decline and indeed, like demand for the whisky to which it gives birth, shows every sign of increasing.

Strathmill
Keith, Banffshire AB55 5DQ.

This distillery is currently owned by Diageo. The water sources are local springs and the distillery produces 1,700,000 litres of malt whisky annually.

In 1891 the present premises were built from the remains of an old corn mill and at first named Glenisla-Glenlivet but four years later it was taken over by the Gilbey company and renamed Strathmill Distillery.

In 1962 it was acquired by UDV and six years later a second pair of stills were added.

In 1975 it was acquired by Grand Metropolitan.

This malt has been an important component of J and B and Dunhill blends.

Glen Isla, which was the first name of this whisky, is in fact down to the south in Angus, being in the valley which cups the upper part of the River Isla. It has nothing to do with Islay, a distilling island far to the south west. There is also a Glenisla village which is around nine miles west of Kirriemuir in Angus.

It was not unknown for whiskies to have Scottish sounding names which in reality had little to do with their geographic locations. The important point was to get over that instant Caledonian association. Some areas, though great distances apart, had similar sounding names anyway.

▶

Tamdhu
Knockando, Aberlour, Banffshire AB38 7RP.

Built in 1896, this distillery closed from 1927 until 1947 but was extended in 1972 from two to four stills and again to six stills three years later.

Sited on the banks of the River Spey in traditional whisky-making country, it is the only distillery to malt all its own barley on site and gets its own water from a spring under the building.

It is currently owned by Ian Macleod Distillers Ltd. and produces four million litres annually.

It was sold to Highland Distilleries Co. Ltd. in 1899.

The distillery was expanded in the 1970s and Tamdhu was launched as a single malt in 1976.

The old railway station at Knockando was then transformed into a visitors' centre.

Many distilleries were once close to railway lines which used to be major facilitators of transport in the more remote stretches of the countryside before the government axe fell on such rural networks in the 1960s.

Whisky makers were forced to use lorries to ferry their goods to major markets on increasingly busy but better developed and maintained roads.

Island distilleries have of course always relied on ships to get their products to the mainland and beyond.

The Tamdhu malt is a major component of Famous Grouse whisky.

Tamnavulin
Tomnavoulin, Banffshire AB37 9JA.

The name means in Gaelic 'the mill on the hill' and the River Livet conveniently flows just past the distillery, which is the only one actually to be built beside the river. The area is a popular picnic spot because of its scenic attributes.

This distillery was built in mid-1960s in order to meet the growing demand from blenders such as Whyte and Mackay's, Crawford's and Mackinley's.

It closed 30 years later but reopened again in the summer of 2007, reverting to the practice of producing a rare single malt whisky. It is still owned by Whyte and Mackay and the water source is springs at nearby Easterton.

The best vintages are 12 and 25 years old.

The current condition of the distillery is officially posted as 'mothballed' but this term in the whisky-making process does not normally mean, as it does in other industries, that everything is closed and nothing is being produced.

Indeed in time-honoured fashion the product made some time ago, namely malt whisky, can still be maturing in the silence and the dark of warehouses and cellars, ready to be revealed at a later date chosen by the distiller who will be keeping a practised, wary eye on the maturation process. The tranquil passing of time is itself part of the production cycle.

The brand name has been simplified from the original Gaelic to make it easier to pronounce, particularly for foreign buyers.

Teaninich
Alness, Ross-shire IV17 OXB.

This distillery is owned by Diageo. The source of water is the nearby Dairywell Spring and this distillery produces 2,700,000 litres of malt whisky annually.

It was founded in 1817 by Captain Hugh Munro and in 1898 was purchased by Elgin-based whisky brokers and merchants, Munro and Cameron.

In 1934 it was taken over by Scottish Malt Distillers Ltd.

In 1962 a second pair of stills were added and in 1971 another still house was built and a further three pairs of stills added.

In 1974 such was the success of the business that the entire building was renovated.

In 1985 the oldest section was closed and refurbished to be reopened six years later.

In 1992 this whisky was first released as a single malt but the majority of production has always gone into blending various other brands.

The best vintages are 10 and 23 years old.

Both Dalmore and Glenmorangie distilleries are close by which makes this a highly-productive area with regards to whisky making.

Teaninich distillery is located in the village of Alness, in eastern Ross and Cromarty, next to the Alness river which rises in the mountains north west of Loch Morie and flows into the Cromarty Firth, so it is situated in ideal whisky making territory.

Some of the church ruins in Alness date back to medieval times but ancient Pictish cairns and standing stones have also been found there.

The whisky brand Teaninich (pronounced Tee-ah-nen-ik) was named after a district in the area whose provenance goes back into the mists of time. It joins a group of several other whisky titles which are difficult to pronounce and which foreigners, who have no knowledge of the Gaelic, in particular find challenging to get their tongues round. ∎

Liquid Gold

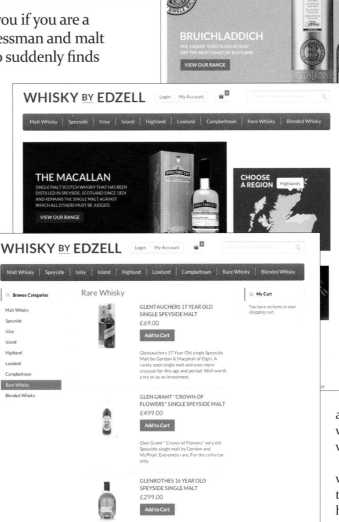

What do you do if you if you are a successful businessman and malt whisky lover who suddenly finds himself with plenty of time on his hands?

In the case of the recently-retired Orry Lovat from Glasgow, you join the growing band of malt whisky investors.

During the current economic slowdown, as returns from traditional markets are proving less attractive, increasing numbers of speculators are turning to whisky in the quest for profits.

For Orry, though, it is more a labour of love – malt has been his favourite drink since he first sampled it at the age of 21.

Aided by his sons, Timothy and Robin, he recently established "Whisky by Edzell" as a vehicle to combine his passion with his proven entrepreneurial skills.

By doing so he has joined many others who are turning Scotland's most famous beverage into liquid gold.

And as Orry explains, there are a number of factors why malt has become such a money magnet.

"Traditionally, malt whisky was produced by small bespoke distilleries. There were no big conglomerates like there are today.

"These myriad small producers only made malt whisky in small quantities.

"From the 1980s onwards there has been a great consolidation in the industry. Many of the original distilleries were swallowed up by the multi-nationals like Diageo, Allied Distillers, Seagram etc.

"Some of these smaller units were closed down because they didn't fit in with the bulk market strategy favoured by the giants of the industry – and much of the malt whisky in their stores was then used as an ingredient in the big-selling blended whisky brands sold by their new owners.

"It meant that many malts would never be produced again and so they became scarcer.

"At the same time mass production and aggressive marketing opened up whisky, blended and malt, to the world, thus stoking demand for both products.

"Consumers in emerging economies like China, Japan, much of South America, India, along with the likes of the USA and Western Europe suddenly got a taste for malt whisky. And although it had always been regarded as a luxury product, millions of people could now afford it for the first time.

"Around five years ago these consumers began searching beyond the big-selling brands. They started looking for the more obscure malts, partly because they could now afford to but also because they were very curious about the various tastes on offer.

"And before long everybody wanted to sample and explore the more obscure malts which had been produced between 1940 and 2000 by these small bespoke distilleries which no longer exist.

"They soon discovered it was very difficult to get hold of this whisky.

"It wasn't available in the shops and anything that hadn't been drunk was in private collections.

"Many of these old collectors have been passing away in recent years and their surviving relatives began looking for a vehicle to dispose of their inheritance.

"Auctioneers cottoned on to this and saw an opportunity to create a new market. They have succeeded beyond their wildest dreams and the prices of these bottles of malt have continued to rise even while other investments have failed.

"There is now a genuine world-wide demand which ensures that the value of these bottles keeps rising. A percentage of it is being drunk by the new owners and this in turn makes the surviving bottles even rarer.

"We started acquiring malt whiskies around five years ago and now have a large collection. We continue to seek old and rare bottles at competitive rates. Some of it we drink, some we keep and others we sell on the open market.

"We now have clients from all over the world."

On their website Orry and his sons offer a variety of single malts ranging from an Old Pulteney 12-year-old at £23.50 to a bottle of Edradour 30-year-old at £1950.

Colin Grant

Master of Malt

Whyte and Mackay's master blender, Richard Paterson, has created a unique single malt whisky which has set new standards for the industry.

The Dalmore King Alexander III, to give it its proper title, is a Highland single malt which can boast six different finishes.

Here we trace its remarkable evolution from conception to completion.

"Back in the early 1990s I was looking for something new," reveals Richard. "I wanted to experiment with single malts, not only to broaden my horizons, but also to stimulate the market.

"I believe part of my raison d'etre is to find new ways for the malt whisky drinker to enjoy his or her dram. The Dalmore is my contribution."

A single malt is traditionally made from a single distillery and most of the time the whisky is left to mature in American white oak barrels.

However, to give the taste an element of elegance and refinement, quite often the product, once matured, will be transferred from American white oak to sherry wood casks and normally it is left there for three years.

Certainly, that used to be the norm.

Richard, though, felt it was time for an alternative approach and began his quest in 1992.

"The King Alexander was born that year and stayed in American white oak where it was stimulated.

"Then we dressed the whisky. Unlike humans who use clothes we dress it with wood.

"This process takes malt whisky to another dimension."

During the next 19 painstaking years Richard worked away with the original Dalmore and tested it in a variety of flavoured barrels.

The exact combination of the end result is a closely-guarded secret but Richard was happy to discuss the ingredients.

"I started out with American white oak, then I used port, Madeira Marsala, Cabernet Sauvignon, small batch bourbon and Matusalem Sherry. The malt was left in these barrels individually, before I mixed everything together at various times until I found the perfect combination.

"It is important to realise that the use of sherry wood does not add sherry to the whisky.

"When I buy a cask in Jerez or La Frontera there are five litres left in it. By the time it reaches Scotland there are only three and then we have to pour out the remainder.

"We are not allowed to add sherry to the whisky, but the sherry lives on in the pores of the wood

"I found that by mixing all these six different finishes I could give malt whisky another dimension. The DNA of the Dalmore still shines through but it is now much more attractive to the connoisseur.

"This is the 1992 Dalmore, although it doesn't say so on the label. It has just been bottled recently, so it is roughly 20 years old. We sell it as a non-age malt at around £120.

"I would describe it as opening a box of chocolates and tasting a multitude of flavours, all the different centres all at the one time.

"The flavours just burst in your mouth – and the longer you keep it in your mouth the more flavour you get. That's what makes it so sensational!"

Colin Grant

Richard spends time in the Sample Room, tasting, blending and

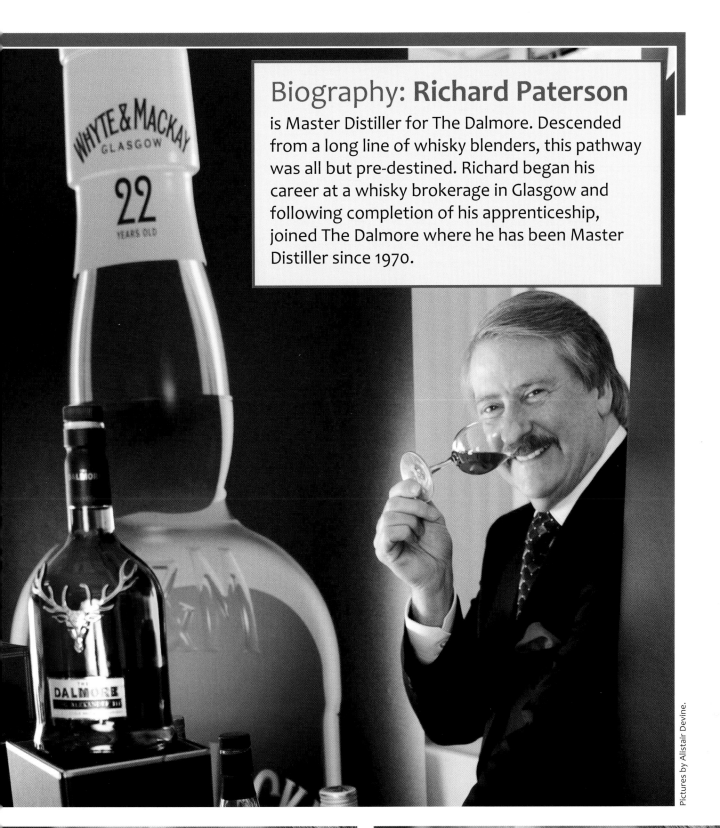

Biography: **Richard Paterson**

is Master Distiller for The Dalmore. Descended from a long line of whisky blenders, this pathway was all but pre-destined. Richard began his career at a whisky brokerage in Glasgow and following completion of his apprenticeship, joined The Dalmore where he has been Master Distiller since 1970.

Pictures by Alistair Devine.

monitoring the various stages of maturation, wood procurement

and implementing innovative proposals for future vattings.

Moonshine in the Glens

Imagine Prohibition America of the Roaring Twenties transferred to the Scottish Highlands and you will get a vague idea of the mayhem that was common during the heydays of whisky smuggling.

The culprits did not have fast cars or machine guns but Illicit Highland distillers were as adept and violent as any 20th century gangster when it came to avoiding the uniformed and armed excisemen who were ordered into the mountains as a Victorian version of the Untouchables.

The origins of the problem arose after the Treaty of Union between Scotland and England in 1707 when, as part of the agreement, English revenue staff crossed the border in a vain attempt to impose some fiscal order onto the collection of taxes levied on thousands of remote whisky stills smoking quietly away in misty, distant locales.

By the end of the 18th century the situation remained so confused that no two distilleries were taxed at he same rate and illicit operations flourished.

The clock tower in the centre of Dufftown once housed a thriving still.

The Highlanders viewed whisky as a gift from God and deeply resented having to pay any revenue to the government of the day for a product which literally (at least when it came to the vital ingredient of water) fell from heaven.

After a lengthy Royal Commission, an Act of 1823 sanctioned legal distilling at a duty of 2/3d per gallon for stills with a capacity of more than 40 gallons.

There was in addition a licence fee of £10 annually and no stills under the legal limit were officially allowed to operate.

The first large scale legitimate distillery came into existence in the following year and thereafter many of the more farsighted distillers, realising that civilisation was rapidly advancing, even into the wild glens, came over to the side of the law in order to get their trade properly codified.

By 1840 the duty was 5d per bottle and the war against bootleggers began in earnest.

However, illicit whisky was not only cheaper but stronger. Men murdered for it, pitched battles were fought over it and fortunes were made and lost through it.

Entire communities were financially decimated by campaigns against smugglers, while some households were destroyed by too much sampling of the liquid product.

Smuggling dens proliferated, from bothies in the Borders to caves on the islands, from pits in the forests to underground hidey-holes on the moors.

Fishermen and farmers quit their hard, dangerous ways of life to participate in the more lucrative black market of illegal hooch.

Some government officers were bribed to turn a blind eye and corruption went as high as the judiciary who often quashed court cases, having illegal whisky in their cellars at home. Some smugglers became so wealthy that they were able to buy large estates in the north.

Various ploys were used to get the illicit product to market. Wives filled pigs' bladders with the liquid and, hanging them from their waists, hid these receptacles under their voluminous skirts.

Contents of casks often bore no relation to labels, while even funerals were sometimes bogus with whisky being packed into the coffins.

If word came from paid informers that the dreaded excisemen were about to mount a raid, a member of the smuggler's family would suddenly be pronounced dead from smallpox or some other equally virulent, contagious disease, thus dissuading any official from making a house search.

Since illicit distilling provided the only vent for the disposal of grain over an extensive area of the Highlands, the landed proprietors and gentlemen farmers could hardly be blamed for encouraging the nefarious goings-on.

Landlords often accepted whisky in payment for overdue rents and it was viewed as a good cure for unemployment and boredom among the more inaccessible tracts of wilderness where only crofting or poaching offered any hazardous alternative.

The vigour and perseverance of the smugglers stood in stark contrast to the apathy and indifference of the authorities but this changed dramatically when the Government hit on the simple idea of appointing Riding Officers who received bonuses for each sizeable seizure.

Nevertheless, the punishment for illegal distilling had little effect on many miscreants who could notch up a couple of dozen offences over a few years and pay small fines without interrupting their lawless business activities.

Diligent excisemen simply doing their duty were killed and wounded, usually by being shot, flung over cliffs or beaten up by mobs as they doggedly went about their unpopular tasks, so that upholding the law became a very dangerous job indeed: but getting witnesses and convictions for these crimes proved almost impossible, such was the unpopularity of officials.

Smugglers too were sometimes shot dead as they tried to escape excisemen; and feelings ran so high in some parts of the Highlands that government officers could not venture into them without the support of troops.

The matter of law and order in the untamed Caledonian wildernesses was raised repeatedly in Parliament with respectable Lowland distillers complaining vociferously that their markets were being destroyed by unfair competition in the north.

It was due to the lobbying of frustrated businessmen, who were losing income, that serious action was eventually taken.

Jail terms and fines were increased and the wages of customs men raised but the Highlanders responded in typical fashion by forming themselves into armed bands that literally harnessed sure-footed ponies to traverse secret mountain tracks down to the southern markets.

George Forbes

Glenlivet became the centre of smuggling activities and the whisky trails were busy with convoys of up to 30 men and their four legged friends heavily laden with casks and sacks containing the golden, liquid product.

Clashes with the authorities often involved gunfire and swordplay with the smugglers melting back into the scenery, carrying away their wounded with them as if from some clan battle of old.

Revenue cutters patrolled the coastline, the Caledonian Canal and sea lochs, checking inter-island transport and commandeering smugglers' boats.

Seizures increased as law enforcement improved in efficiency; and by the end of the 19th century illegal distilling on an industrial scale had been effectively stamped out.

Great ingenuity and daring was used to avoid the payment of tax and even today occasional casks can be unearthed in unlikely places.

For instance, old stills were found under the Free Tron Church in Edinburgh's High Street and also under an arch of that city's South Bridge and buried in the walls of a Leith close.

Other locations have included next door to the Customs House in Aberdeen, sheep dips, mountain caverns and deep underneath many existing distilleries.

The clock tower in the centre of Dufftown once housed a thriving still which the local exciseman passed every day on his way to work.

At various lochs smugglers used to attach a cord and small float to their equipment before committing it to the watery depths from where it could easily be pulled up.

At Nigg in Ross-shire the local smugglers enjoyed the active support of the church beadle who willingly lodged their still underneath the pulpit in return for a good, regular dram.

But usually the nearest moor or heather-clad hillside offered hiding places galore.

The market for immature, bootleg whisky effectively dried up in the face of plentiful supplies of legally distilled spirits of steadily improving quality and availability.

The financial attractions of working in a legitimate, lucrative trade began to look rosier to the natives of the Highlands succumbing to the advances of progress as opposed to the riskier and haphazard past ways of the old smuggling life.

By the Edwardian age, excise seizures almost entirely involved small isolated stills and the death blow was dealt to the smugglers when the use of barley as a foodstuff became a matter of national security during the First World War.

Hysterical alarms about drunkenness among the general population and ammunition workers in particular led to much more stringent rules with regards to the creation and consumption of alcoholic liquors and any lawbreaking was ruthlessly dealt with as opposed to a measure of leniency prevalent in previous decades.

Nowadays few people have the knowledge or skills needed to distil an invigorating spirit; so the the chances of the colourful days of the whisky smugglers ever returning are remote.

It was a wild, adventurous time when many of the best qualities of the Scots, like initiative, courage, inventiveness and defiance, were used in the service of yet another lost cause. ∎

THE LAST ILLICIT DISTILLER IN THE HIGHLANDS

The final illegal distillery put together on a scale large enough to provide a major income was that belonging to Hamish Dhu Macrae in Monar at the head of Glen Strathfarrar on the county border of Inverness-shire and Ross and Cromarty.

This was a remote spot once only accessible via a drove road and Hamish duly set about supporting his wife and family by cultivating a few acres of barley and potatoes beside a loch with a makeshift dam.

Using his cottage as a base and the surrounding peaks as look-out points complete with telescopes, Hamish proceeded to make whisky in the winter which was then distributed during the summer.

As well as locals, including lairds who turned a blind – and bleary – eye to his activities, Hamish supplied hostelries, safe in the knowledge that the nearest government outpost was 40 miles away over very rough terrain.

His home was so difficult to approach surreptitiously, even by the late 19th century, that warnings could easily be sent ahead about the laborious incursions of excisemen and suitable action thus taken.

On one occasion the redcoat raiders were escorted by crofters en route to some typically generous Highland hospitality and got so drunk they were put to bed. They were then so ill in the morning that they gave up trying to catch Hamish red handed and returned home.

But by 1900 there were a lot fewer illicit stills to close down and the knot was tightening around Hamish.

He was eventually talked into giving up his illegal activities by one of his best customers, Captain Stirling, proprietor of the Monar estate, who knew such illegal activities were now outdated.

Yet Hamish retained some shrewd native devilry. He went to Beauly market where he had often sold his illegal wares and informed the customs men there that he could pinpoint an illegal still for them as long as he received his just reward of £5, then the government's current payment for such a civic duty (this sum being large by the standards of the day).

Hamish then led them to his very own still in a 'secret' bothy, stating that he had been shocked – shocked! – when he literally stumbled across it.

Thus illicit distilling ended as it had thrived – through trickery and subterfuge.

Whisky Galore – The Real Story

DVD cover of the Ealing film classic.

Most people have enjoyed the 1949 Ealing comedy 'Whisky Galore' and have laughed at the antics of the Hebridean islanders and their efforts to outwit the authorities by stealing a cargo of whisky wrecked on their island; and a lot of viewers believe the film a work of fiction.

In fact it is based on solid fact and the author of the original comic novel, Sir Compton Mackenzie, had a holiday home in the area where the hilarious events occurred.

It all began with the 8,000 ton SS *Politician* (in the film she is called the *Cabinet Minister*) beating through a storm in the treacherous Minch during early February, 1941.

This was a critical time in the Second World War when beleaguered, rationed Britain, standing alone against the Nazis, was cash strapped and keen to sell exports abroad to raise some much needed revenue.

With this in mind, the *Politician's* hold was packed full of luxury goods bound for America, including 28,000 cases of whisky containing 264,000 full bottles of the best malt available.

The ship was in difficulty weathering a gale in high seas when she suddenly struck a reef off the Outer Hebridean island of Eriskay and had to be abandoned.

It did not take the islanders, who were used to extending hospitality to shipwrecked mariners, long to find out what exactly the cargo was – and so the fun began.

Islanders were adept at plundering wrecks off their rocky, perilous shores and it could prove lucrative if hazardous work.

Just as portrayed in the film, they began to ransack the vessel and the local home guard officer, who wanted to mount a patrol to protect the precious cargo until the authorities arrived, was duly kidnapped by the wily islanders and locked in a local croft far away from the wreck.

While the *Politician's* unharmed crew were hastily ferried south to safety, it took the coastguards, police, salvage experts and excisemen weeks to get organized.

Meanwhile, alerted raiders from all over the islands mounted nautical expeditions on the wreck perched precariously on the reef.

Continuing bad weather hindered official efforts to retrieve what could be got from the floundering vessel but a bit of wind and rain did not stop the redoubtable and thirsty islanders who were used to such inclement conditions and anyway were quite prepared to take risks during the winter nights for the rewards on offer.

These raiders often held impromptu parties of their own involving drinking, singing and dancing on board the stricken and abandoned vessel since they had gone years without imbibing their proper supplies of drams and simply could not wait until getting back to shore.

Some even wore their wives' clothing to avoid incriminating oil getting on their own apparel.

And, just as in the book and film, many ingenious hiding places had to be found for the stolen whisky, the most popular venues including caves and holes in the ground with suitable landmarks nearby.

A few islanders were caught bottle in hand and jailed for a few weeks but the majority managed to enjoy their stolen gains without interference.

The local police were less than enthusiastic about enforcing the law anyway since they had all been bribed by free bottles.

There was even a real life Captain Wagget, an officious outsider keen to uphold law and order whose pomposity was the source of much merriment in both book and film as well as in reality where he was customs officer Charles McColl, a stickler for the rules and righteously enraged by all the thievery going on around him.

McColl got his revenge by eventually exploding the hull of the wreck while the islanders looked on in dismay, their attitude summed up by Angus John Campbell who exclaimed angrily, " Dynamiting whisky – you wouldn't think there'd be men in the world as crazy as that!"

And so the waves eventually lapped over the wreck, consigning her and what was left of her cargo to the deep.

But the incident's heritage lived on in folklore and the fertile mind of a comic writer; and years later the first pub on Eriskay was of course called the Politician and had some of the dusty old bottles from the wreck on the gantry, not to be drunk of course but to be paid due reverence by the customers.

George Forbes